On Order

Other Titles of Interest from St. Augustine's Press

St. Augustine, *The St. Augustine LifeGuide: Words to Live by from the Great Christian Saint.* Translated by Silvano Borruso

Aristotle, *Physics, Or Natural Hearing.* Translated by Glen Coughlin

Aristotle, *Aristotle – On Poetics.* Translated by Seth Benardete and Michael Davis

Michael Davis, *The Poetry of Philosophy*

Plato, *The Symposium of Plato: The Shelley Translation.* Translated by Percy Bysshe Shelley

Thomas Aquinas, *Commentary on Aristotle's Nicomachean Ethics*

Thomas Aquinas, *Commentary on Aristotle's De Anima*

Thomas Aquinas, *Commentary on Aristotle's Metaphysics*

Thomas Aquinas, *Commentary on Aristotle's Posterior Analytics*

Thomas Aquinas, *Commentary on Aristotle's Physics*

Thomas Aquinas, *Disputed Questions on Virtue.* Translated by Ralph McInerny

Thomas Aquinas, *Commentary on the Epistle to the Hebrews.* Translated by Chrysostom Baer, O. Praem.

Thomas Aquinas, *Commentaries on St. Paul's Epistles to Timothy, Titus, and Philemon.* Translated by Chrysostom Baer, O. Praem.

John of St. Thomas, *Introduction to the Summa Theologiae of Thomas Aquinas.* Translated by Ralph McInerny

Seth Benardete, *Sacred Transgressions: A Reading of Sophocles' Antigone*

Josef Pieper, *Leisure, the Basis of Culture*

Josef Pieper, *Scholasticism: Personalities and Problems*

Josef Pieper, *The Silence of St. Thomas*

Francisco Suarez, *On Creation, Conservation, & Concurrence: Metaphysical Disputations 20–22.* Translated by A.J. Freddoso

Francisco Suarez, *Metaphysical Demonstration of the Existence of God.* Translated by John P. Doyle

Leo Strauss, *Xenophon's Socrates*

Leo Strauss, *Xenophon's Socratic Discourse: An Interpretation of the Oeconomicus*

Ronna Burger, *The Phaedo: A Platonic Labyrinth*

Stanley Rosen, *Plato's Sophist: The Drama of Original and Image*

Stanley Rosen, *Plato's Symposium*

Stanley Rosen, *Plato's Statesman*

Stanley Rosen, *The Ancients and the Moderns: Rethinking Modernity*

On Order
[*De Ordine*]

St. Augustine

Translation and introduciton by
Silvano Borruso

St. Augustine's Press
South Bend, Indiana
2007

Manufactured in the United States of America.

1 2 3 4 5 12 11 10 09 08 07

Library of Congress Cataloging in Publication Data
Augustine, Saint, Bishop of Hippo.
[De ordine. English & Latin]
On order [de ordine] St. Augustine; translated and introduced by Silvano Borruso.
p. cm.
Other title: De ordine
Facing text in Latin and English.
Includes index.
ISBN 1-58731-603-X (clothbound: alk. paper)
1. Providence and government of God. 2. Good and evil. I. Title: De ordine. II. Title.
BR65.A6975E5 2007
117 – dc22 2005029433

∞ The paper used in this publication meets the minimum requirements of the American National Standard for Information Sciences – Permanence of Paper for Printed Materials, ANSI Z39.48-1984.

St. Augustine's Press
www.staugustine.net

Contents

Introduction

Historical background

It is November 386. Augustine, 32, is a fresh convert from a dreary lifestyle of heresy and lust that has left him first disgusted and now exhausted. He has run away from his post of teaching rhetoric in Milan and has retreated to the villa of his friend Verecundus at Cassiciacum near Milan.

Monica, 55, his mother, is with him. Her prayers and penance have obtained her son's conversion, dreamed of ever since he had begun to fall for the temptations of Carthage a decade and a half earlier. He would be baptized by Bishop St. Ambrose on Holy Saturday 387. Monica, a most lovable character as she appears in the course of the debates, is unaware that her mission on earth is at an end. She would not see her native Africa again, dying at Ostia on the eve of their re-embarking for Carthage before the end of 387.

The firebrand Licentius, a teenager, son of Augustine's friend Romanianus, is perhaps the most interesting character of *De Ordine*. He appears mesmerized by the beauty and coherence of philosophical endeavor, and does not hesitate to put his thinking at the mercy of Augustine's thrusts.

Trygetius is a veteran just retired from the Roman army. He is obviously older than Licentius. He speaks little, but when he does he speaks undoubted sense.

Alypius is an old friend, of Augustine's age. They are both natives of Tagaste (today Souk-Ahras, Algeria) in North Africa. They had fallen into and risen from heresy together. The two would end as bishops: Augustine at Hippo Regius (today Annaba, Algeria) and Alypius at Tagaste his native city.

Navigius is Augustine's brother. He is present, but does not take part in the debate.

The two books are written in dialogue form, following a classical tradition immortalized by Plato (427–347 B.C.).

To complete the historical background it is necessary to mention that Siricius was pope in Rome that year. He condemned the Manicheans, the very sect which had allured young Augustine into heresy for many years. Theodosius the Great was reigning at Constantinople as emperor of the East, while the West was being disputed between claimants and counter-claimants. Theodosius is responsible for having cleaved the empire into East and West with a line bearing his name and passing smack in the middle of what is today Bosnia.

Milan had been the imperial capital of the West since the administrative reform by Diocletian ninety years earlier. It was from there that Constantine had issued the Edict of 313 allowing the free practice of the Christian faith. In 330 he had founded Constantinople, for more than a thousand years the most Christian city in the world.

The year 1986 saw the 1600th anniversary of Augustine's conversion, and concomitantly, of *De Ordine*. On that occasion, Pope John Paul II issued the Apostolic Letter *Augustinum Hipponensem*, recommended reading for anyone who wants to digest in a few pages the life and works of the great bishop, Father and Doctor of the Church.

There is only one mention of *De Ordine* in the entire letter, but there is something more: St. Augustine practiced what he preached, and Pope John Paul describes it as follows:

> In his diocese, which he never left except in the case of necessity, he was assiduous in preaching – he preached on Saturday and Sunday, and frequently throughout the entire week; – in catechesis; in what he called "the bishop's audience," which sometime lasted for an entire day, so that he did not eat; in the care of the poor; in the formation of the clergy; in directing the monks, many of whom were later called to the priesthood and the episcopate, and in the guidance of the monasteries of nuns. When he died, "he left the Church a very numerous clergy, and monasteries of men and women full of those consecrated to chastity under their superiors, and libraries."[1]

1 *Augustinum Hipponensem*, III 240–48

Augustine, in other words, *lived* order: he did not confine himself to writing about it.

De Ordine is a work of youthful maturity. Augustine's life would span forty-four years more. Towards the close of his life he wrote the famous *Retractationes*, in which he expressed regret at some of the things he had affirmed many years earlier. A few of them regard *De Ordine*, and they will be mentioned in the appropriate places.

Cultural background

Augustine's classical education was steeped in pagan lore. It is not possible to understand some of his points without at least an idea of the stories he mentions in the course of the debate.

Close to the beginning (I 6) there is mention of Licentius's Muse. In II 41 he mentions the Muses again as daughters of Jupiter and Mnemosyne (Greek for memory). The myth is that after the defeat of the Titans the gods asked Zeus to beget divinities to celebrate the victory of the Olympian gods. Zeus readily complied. Attracted by Mnemosyne in one of his fathering jaunts, he begat the nine Muses by her on nine consecutive nights.

They were Clio (history), Euterpe (wind instruments), Thalia (comedy), Melpomene (tragedy), Terpsichore (lyric poetry and dance), Erato (love poetry), Polyhymnia (mime), Urania (astronomy), and Calliope (epic poetry and rhetoric). In the *Retractationes* Augustine regretted having taken the Muses seriously. He must be turning in his grave to see what some people take seriously *today*.

Mount Helicon (I 8) is the mountain where the Muses dwelled in preference to Olympus, the abode of the other gods.

The legend of Pyramus and Thisbe (I 8, 12 and 21) comes from book IV of Ovid's *Metamorphoses*. They were young lovers living in Nineveh, who after sleepless nights talking to each other through a crack in the wall dividing their homes, decided on a night rendezvous by the tomb of Ninus, the legendary founder of the city.

Thisbe arrived first, but who arrived second was not Pyramus. It was a thirsty lioness, fresh from a kill of some cattle. Thisbe ran away in terror, leaving behind her shawl, which the lioness chewed up and trampled upon on its way to water.

When Pyramus arrived, he did not find his lover, but her shawl. Putting two and two together, he got three instead of four, and decided that life was not worth living without her. He drew his sword and plunged it into his heart.

Then Thisbe got out of her hiding place, only to find Pyramus exhale his last in a pool of blood. The rest is the typical dénouement of a Greek (or Assyrian) tragedy: she fell on Pyramus's sword and killed herself.

Augustine mentions a double Apollo in I 10. This reflects the confusion of many mythological stories. In Greek mythology Apollo appears as sun-god, shepherd-god, musician, builder, and colonizing god. No one has sorted out the confusion, and this is clearly not the place to do so.

The myth of Daedalus and his son Icarus makes a brief appearance in II 37. Daedalus was a legendary engineer, the designer of the famous labyrinth (maze) for King Minos of Crete. It was he who gave Ariadne the ball of thread by which she was able to get out of the labyrinth. For this slip Minos locked father and son in it, but they built wings and flew off. Icarus, however, went too close to the sun, which melted the wax holding the feathers onto the wings. Icarus was killed.

In II 37 Augustine mentions Euryalus. The character is from Virgil's Aeneid (V 294). Euryalus' two claims to fame are his beauty, and his having won a foot race by a clever fouling of his friend Nisus. Virgil names his father Opheltes, but not his mother. Augustine refers to what must have been a standing joke among the *literati* of his day. Not to know Euryalus's mother was to be ignorant of the Aeneid, but to feel piqued at being asked and to call the questioner names was to make a fool of oneself for not getting the joke.

Venus and Cupid are the Latin names of the two most important Greek gods of love: Aphrodite and Eros, mother and son. They appear twice in the text (I 21 and II 34). The second time they are spoken of as impersonated by an actor. Modern readers may wonder why a man should impersonate a woman. The reason is that acting in ancient times was a hazard not unlike war. Murder on the stage was resorted to occasionally, and the crowd

loved it. Women were not allowed to act for the same reason that they were not allowed to fight: men are expendable; women are not.

Proteus (II 43), son of Oceanus and Thethys, was a marine god, coming out of the water every day at noon to rest on a rock. He never spoke unless forced to, in which case he always spoke the truth. The problem was to catch him, for he would change shape at will to escape interrogation. Hence the reference to him by Alypius in his debate against the Academicians.

Besides mythology, Augustine quotes and mentions historical characters.

Zenobius, the friend to whom he dedicates *De Ordine*.

Theodore Manlius, another friend, a minor author whom Augustine praises to the skies in I 9. In the *Retractationes* he considered that praise rather extravagant.

Terence (Publius Terentius Afer, 190–159 BC). He was from Carthage (near Tunis, North Africa) the same part of the world as Augustine and his friends. He was a liberated slave who became a comic poet. He is quoted in I 9.

Virgil (Publius Vergilius Maro, 70–19 BC), of whose works Augustine was so fond (I 26), is without question the greatest of Latin poets. His works still serve as texts wherever people have had the sense of keeping Latin.

Varro (Marcus Terentius, 116–27 BC) is mentioned in II 35 and 54. He was a famous author and historian. In Augustine's times perhaps most of his works were extant. Few are today.

Pythagoras (fl.6th century BC) was the founder of the religious philosophical school that held number to be the principle of all things. Augustine seems to be taken by the idea (II 54), but in the *Retractationes* he regretted having lavished such praise on Pythagoras.

Marcus Tullius Cicero (106–43 BC) is mentioned twice: for having saved Rome from the Catiline conspiracy and for his mastery of the Latin language (II 22 & 45).

All in all, Augustine is well planted on tradition. His familiarity with texts of more than 400 years of age prove that he was no seeker after fashion. If, despite the above attempt at expounding

on classical tradition, modern readers find Book One boring, they may directly tackle Book Two, where Augustine's unsurpassed genius will surely rivet their attention.

Philosophy

Despite taking much from Plato and referring to the Aristotelian categories (II 44), Augustine does not mention either philosopher by name in the whole work. Plato gets one mention in the *Retractationes*.

From the first three debates it is clear that Augustine's attempt at defining and discussing order is not a happy one. There is some fumbling, especially in the unclear, when not unsavory, consequences that flow from the definitions.

Let us try to understand. We are near the end of the fourth century. Justin, Tertullian, Lactantius, Minucius Felix, Arnobius, and other Christian apologists have long ago broken a lance in defense of the Christian faith, but they have not developed a systematic, all-encompassing *philosophical terminology*.

It would not happen for another eight centuries. Had Augustine and friends been acquainted with Thomas Aquinas' *De Ente et Essentia*, they would not have tried to define order as univocally as they did.

By the Aristotelian categories, order is a *relation of finalities*, and therefore not a substance, but an accident. As only substances have a true essence, so only they enjoy a true definition. Accidents, St. Thomas points out, can only be defined in relation to the substance in which they inhere. And here is where Augustine and friends get into trouble.

In *De Ordine*, the Augustinian view of philosophy does not differ much from the Thomist one. Both have it that philosophy is the love of wisdom, and wisdom is none other than the ability to order things according to purpose. Augustine deems the two fields of God and the human soul sufficient to encompass that wisdom (II 16–17 & 47). This is fair enough, but passing from one field into the other is an exercise in *analogy*, an idea well ahead of its time at the end of the fourth century. The *term* "order" is the same in both fields, but behind it there lurk two *vastly different realities*.

Hence the unsatisfactory result that made Augustine retract almost the whole idea of *De Ordine*:

> When I saw that the subject, difficult indeed to understand, could not by disputation be brought to the comprehension of those with whom I was debating, I preferred to talk about an *Order of Study*, by which one can advance from corporeal things to the incorporeal.[2]

Otherwise the Augustinian world-view appears as a solid foundation on which the philosophy of the Schools would rely centuries later, as the examples below will show.

Very early on (I 31) the point is clearly made that philosophy is the preserve of *free* men and women, the latter surprisingly getting place of honor in the person of the lovable Monica. This is no less true today, and in need of great stressing. Far from Augustine's inquiry are pompous abstractions and academic volatilities. Everything is grist to his philosophical mill: from earthly (and earthy) cockfights to the heavens above, passing through public executioners and ladies of the twilight, philosophy acquires an unexpected human dimension.

The senses and the mind are each given their due (II 5 & 32), with very telling examples especially of vision and hearing (II 32). The adequacy of person and method to the thing to be learned is constantly emphasized. The Schools built their world view on this solid foundation, until its demise at the hands of William of Ockham (c.1300–1349) to whom the confusion of modern philosophy is largely due.

Order stands out the more, when seeded with a sprinkle (but just a sprinkle) of disorder. The delightful example of II 13 on the moderate use of slang and solecism is to the point. This can be taken as the basis for the realistic ethical principle of and-and, rather than the rationalistic one of either-or. It is the same with the social order, from which disorder cannot be eliminated, but within which it can be monitored (II 12).

2 St. Augustine's *Retractationes*, in *Divine Providence and the Problem of Evil*. A translation of St. Augustine's *De Ordine*, by Robert P. Russell, O.S.A., Ph.D. (New York: Cosmopolitan 1942), p.176.

Augustine is definitely not a specialist, that plague of modernity. In II 15 he advocates instruction in all branches of learning to stimulate one's mind into appreciating order. It stands to reason: focusing one's attention on a single issue prevents seeing how it is connected to other issues. The specialist, in other words, perennially risks knowing without understanding, and by choice at that!

His analogy of the circle (I 3) and his equaling the center of the circle with the Trinity (II 16) identify the modern disorder in higher education. The university, that originally Catholic institution, lost its center with the abolition of theology. As a result, the university has become hardly distinguishable from a technical school, the more mind-impoverishing, the more specialized it is.

Augustine is no egalitarian. Giving fools their due, he spells out the order of learning and the right method in II 25. No use trying without inner intellectual and moral order. This prescription may come as a shock to those accustomed to the oft-repeated canard that anyone, given enough time and training, can learn or do anything. But it is a salutary shock, a good piece of advice coming from the wisdom of the ancient world.

Confusion infiltrates again in the question of evil. There is only one reference to evil being nothing (II 23), but the point remains undeveloped. Most of the discussion gives the impression that evil is something. The elements for setting everything in its place are there, but the point that evil is aversion from order born of a misdirected non-divine intelligence is never made. He even speaks of a "nature" of evil (II 46). St. Thomas would sort out the question in his definitive *De Malo*.

De Ordine is, when all is said and done, Augustine's own introduction to philosophy, in a sweeping bird's-eye view of what it is to reproduce in one's inner being the double order of things (intellect) and loves (will) existing in the real universe. We can hardly blame him for not achieving, let alone exhausting, the issue, but it is easy to speak with an added wisdom of sixteen centuries. Augustine's achievement is all the more impressive for having achieved what he did when he did it.

Relevance of *De Ordine* today

It is debatable whether the disorder gripping the world at the

beginning of the third millennium is greater or less than that depicted in *De Ordine*.

In the matter of civil disturbances Augustine mentions a riot (I 20) in which his mother Monica had actually taken place not long before. She had spent days and nights singing and praying in the cathedral of Milan to prevent the Arians from taking it over. The Western Roman Empire was tottering. The British legions had elected emperor Maximus, who would be assassinated scarcely a year after the writing of *De Ordine*. Less than a century later, the Western Empire would be no more.

We all know what the twentieth century has wrought in the history of the world, but a comparison blow by blow with the fourth would be too much to undertake here. The relevance of *De Ordine* is that if Augustine was able to write such a masterpiece in the midst of all *that*, there is no reason why a serious student of philosophy should not strive to achieve order in mind and heart in the midst of all *this*.

What has lost not an iota of relevance is his advice to young people on what to do with themselves. Apart from avoiding foolishness, ignorance, and pride, he more specifically exhorts them to shun vice, not to desire public office before time, and to prepare themselves for it with a hard life. He spells out the importance of the liberal arts, sadly neglected today by all so-called educational "systems," but as important as ever in real education. Conclusion: following St. Augustine instead of a conventional "syllabus" would give any talented youth a better education than years of drudgery at the desk of a conventional school.

In I 30 and II 29 he mentions peer pressure and the evil of rivalry for its own sake. These particular disorders do not affect youth exclusively. The economics of envy makes full use of both, prodding people into getting into permanent debt just to conform. The liberating power of truth must be experienced to be appreciated, and *De Ordine* is as good a starting place as any.

The Translation

De Ordine was first translated into English in 1942, in the United States, by Fr. Robert P. Russell, appropriately of the order of St. Augustine.

Whether or not other translations have appeared in the 65 years since, a new one is offered to lovers of philosophy and of Augustine.

Rather than following the original Latin as closely as Russell, I have opted for putting in St. Augustine's mouth (and pen) expressions which I think he would use were he to speak English today. I have not, I hope, made him say what he did not, or omitted what he clearly did say.

For the sake of clarity I have rendered the dialogue in modern form, eliminating all the "I said," "he said," and putting the initials of the debaters instead.

To avoid footnotes and excuses as to why I translated certain expressions one way and not another, I offer the original Latin side-by-side with the translation.

The Latin text is that of the Benedictines of the 1942 Russell translation. This has been checked against the Migne as downloaded from www.augustinus.it. Resulting discrepancies have been further checked against the 1986 Doignon text, kindly supplied by Dr. Richard Upsher Smith of the Franciscan University of Steubenville, Ohio.

Silvano Borruso
28th August 2006
Feast of St. Augustine

On Order
[*De Ordine*]

LIBER PRIMUS

DISPUTATIO PRIMA

CAPUT I
Omnia divina Providentia regit

1. Ordinem rerum, Zenobi, consequi ac tenere cuique proprium, tum vero universitatis quo coercetur ac regitur hic mundus, vel videre vel pandere difficillimum hominibus atque rarissimum est. Huc accedit quod etiamsi quis haec possit, non illud quoque valet efficere, ut dignum auditorem tam divinis obscurisque rebus, vel vitae merito vel habitu quodam eruditionis inveniat. Nec tamen quidquam est quod magis avide expetant quaeque optima ingenia magisque audire ac discere studeant, qui scopulos vitae huius et procellas, velut erecto quantum licet capite, inspiciunt, quam quomodo fiat ut et Deus humana curet et tanta in humanis rebus perversitas usquequaque diffusa sit, ut non divinae, sed ne servili quidem cuipiam procurationi, si ei tanta potestas daretur, tribuenda esse videatur. Quamobrem illud quasi necessarium iis quibus talia sunt curae, credendum dimittitur, aut divinam providentiam non usque in haec ultima et ima pertendi aut certe mala omnia Dei voluntate committi.

Utrumque impium, sed magis posterius. Quamquam enim desertum Deo quidquam credere cum imperitissimum tum etiam periculosissimum animo sit, tamen in ipsis hominibus nemo quemquam non potuisse aliquid criminatus est; neglegentiae vero vituperatio multo est quam malitiae crudelitatisque purgatior. Itaque velut compellitur ratio tenere non immemor pietatis aut ista terrena non posse a divinis administrari aut negligi atque contemni potius quam ita gubernari, ut omnis de Deo sit mitis atque inculpanda conquestio.

2. Sed quis tamen caecus est mente, ut quidquam in movendis corporibus rationis quod praeter humanam dispositionem ac voluntatem est, divinae potentiae moderationique dare dubitet? Nisi forte, aut casibus tam rata subtilique dimensione vel minutissimorum quorumque animalium membra figurantur aut quod casu

BOOK ONE

FIRST DEBATE

ONE
Divine Providence rules all

1. There is an order to be found, within things and between them, which binds and directs this world. To attain and retain that order, Zenobius, to open one's eyes and other people's to it, it is difficult and very uncommon. Even one who has the ability for it will not necessarily succeed. One needs to find worthy listeners with an ordered lifestyle and an ordered mind to grasp such divine but obscure realities. Neither is it sufficient to be eager to listen and learn. No sooner does one lift one's head enough to pay attention to the obstacles and difficulties of life, than it comes natural to ask how it is that on the one hand God takes care of human affairs, and on the other these same affairs are shot through with so much evil. Not even an administration of slaves, given authority and power, could perpetrate as much. Those who find themselves in such straits come to one of two conclusions: either the power of divine providence does not quite reach the deeper limits of things, or such evils happen because God wills them.

Both are godless conclusions, especially the second. To deem anything forsaken by God is both ignorant and most dangerous. Not even civil society blames anyone for incapacity, but it rightly condemns negligence, more lightly for sure than malice or cruelty. Reason then, despite the promptings of piety, comes to think that earthly things are outside God's control, or that He neglects or despises them. It fails to see how well-governed they are, and that complaining against God is neither a trifling exercise nor one free from blame.

2. Who is so mentally blind as to doubt that whatever controls the motion of bodies, way beyond human understanding and will, does not really depend on God's direction and power? One could, of course, attribute to chance such a finely tuned proportion of parts down to that of the minutest animals. Deny chance, and the

quis negat, possit nisi ratione factum fateri aut vero per universam naturam, quod in singulis quibusque rebus nihil arte humana satagente ordinatum miramur, alienare a secretissimo maiestatis arbitrio ullis nugis vanae opinionis audebimus. At enim hoc ipsum est plenius quaestionum, quod membra pulicis disposita mire atque distincta sunt, cum interea humana vita innumerabilium perturbationum inconstantia versetur et fluctuet.

Sed hoc pacto si quis tam minutum cerneret, ut in vermiculato pavimento nihil ultra unius tessellae modulum acies eius valeret ambire, vituperaret artificem velut ordinationis et compositionis ignarum eo quod varietatem lapillorum perturbatam putaret, a quo illa emblemata in unius pulchritudinis faciem congruentia simul cerni collustrarique non possent. Nihil enim aliud minus eruditis hominibus accidit, qui universam rerum coaptationem atque concentum imbecilla mente complecti et considerare non valentes, si quid eos offenderit, quia suae cogitationi magnum est, magnam putant rebus inhaerere foeditatem.

3. Cuius erroris maxima causa est, quod homo sibi ipse est incognitus. Qui tamen ut se noscat, magna opus habet consuetudine recedendi a sensibus et animum in seipsum colligendi atque in seipso retinendi. Quod ii tantum assequuntur, qui plagas quasdam opinionum, quas vitae quotidianae cursus infligit, aut solitudine inurunt aut liberalibus medicant disciplinis.

CAPUT II
Dedicat hoc opus Zenobio

Ita enim animus sibi redditus, quae sit pulchritudo universitatis intellegit, quae profecto ab *uno* cognominata est. Idcircoque illam videre non licet animae quae in multa procedit sectaturque aviditate pauperiem, quam nescit sola segregatione multitudinis posse vitari. Multitudinem autem non hominum dico, sed omnium quae sensus attingit. Nec mirere quod eo egestatem patitur magis, quo magis appetit plura complecti. Ut enim in circulo quantumvis amplo unum est medium quo cuncta convergunt,

only alternatives are either to admit the fact of a guiding reason, or to submit to the inane, vain opinion of those who dare subtract the government of the universe from the secret designs of God, in spite of human powerlessness to control even its smallest component. But this poses even more problems, namely how to account for the astonishing order of the smallest joints of a flea, together with the ups and downs of endless disorder afflicting human life.

The situation is akin to that of one who, confined to surveying a single section of a mosaic floor, looked at it too closely, and then blamed the artisan for being ignorant of order and composition. In reality it is he himself who, in concentrating on an apparently disordered variety of small colored cubes, failed to notice the larger mosaic work. The apparent disorder of the elements really comes together into the unity of a beautiful portrait. The same can be said of the feeble-minded ignoramus. Unable to grasp the harmony and interaction of the universe as a whole, and hurt by what is beyond their ken, such people rashly conclude that things are inherently ugly and disorderly.

3. The main cause of this error is the lack of knowledge of self. In order to know oneself it is most necessary to get out of the life of the senses into one's interior, and there recollect oneself. Some cauterize the wound of disordered opinion inflicted on them in day-to-day life by retreating into solitude. Others do the same by cultivating the liberal arts.

TWO
Dedicates the work to Zenobius

The human spirit, recollected within itself, grasps the beauty of the universe, which gets its name from *unum in diversis*, one in many. Therefore that vision is denied to the soul distracted by too many pursuits, which avidly attains nothing but poverty. Only by separating oneself from the crowd can one avoid it. Crowd not of people, mind you, but of material things. Don't be surprised that one is the poorer, the more one desires to be encircled by such things. However great a circumference is, there is a single point of

quod *centrum* geometrae vocant, et quamvis totius ambitus partes innumerabiliter secari queant, nihil tamen est praeter illud unum, quo cetera pariliter dimetiantur et quod omnibus quasi quodam aequalitatis iure dominetur; hinc vero in quamlibet partem si egredi velis, eo amittuntur omnia, quo in plurima pergitur: sic animus a seipso fusus immensitate quadam diverberatur et vera mendicitate conteritur, cum eum natura sua cogit ubique unum quaerere et multitudo invenire non sinit.

4. Sed et haec quae dixi qualia sint et quae causa exstet erroris animarum, quoque modo et in unum congruant atque perfecta sint cuncta et tamen peccata fugienda sint, assequeris profecto, mi Zenobi. Sic enim mihi notum est ingenium tuum et pulchritudinis omnimodae amator animus, sine libidinis immoderatione atque sordibus. Quod signum in te futurae sapientiae perniciosis cupiditatibus divino iure praescribit, ne tuam causam deseras falsis voluptatibus illectus, qua praevaricatione nihil turpius et periculosius inveniri potest. Assequeris ergo ista, mihi crede, cum eruditionis operam dederis, qua purgatur et excolitur animus, nullo modo ante idoneus cui divina semina committantur.

Quod totum cuiusmodi sit et quem flagitet ordinem, quidve studiosis et bonis ratio promittat, qualemque vitam nos vivamus carissimi tui, et quem fructum de liberali otio carpamus, hi te libri satis, ut opinor, edocebunt, nomine tuo nobis quam nostra elaboratione dulciores, praesertim si te in ipsum ordinem, de quo ad te scribo, meliora eligens inserere atque coaptare volueris.

5. Nam cum stomachi dolor scholam me deserere coegisset, qui iam, ut scis, etiam sine ulla tali necessitate in philosophiam confugere moliebar, statim me contuli ad villam familiarissimi nostri Verecundi. Quid dicam, eo libente? Nosti optime hominis cum in omnes, tum vero in nos benevolentiam singularem. Ibi disserebamus inter nos quaecumque videbantur utilia, adhibito sane stilo quo cuncta exciperentur, quod videbam conducere valetudini meae. Cum enim nonnulla loquendi cura detinerer, nulla inter disputandum irrepebat immoderata contentio. Simul etiam ut si quid

convergence, the *center*. The circumference can be divided and subdivided, but not the center. Everything in a circle refers to the center and is ruled by it as it were. In whatever direction you move from the center, the more diversity you pursue, the more unity you lose. Equally the human spirit, let loose from itself, gets more and more dispersed by the immense variety of things, and as a result oppressed by a true beggar's indigence. By its very nature the human spirit is impelled to seek unity everywhere, but is prevented from attaining it by the crowding of things.

4. Surely you understand, Zenobius, the nature of what I spoke about: the main cause of human error, the tendency towards a natural unity in everything that is, and the need for fleeing from sin. For I know your character. You, a lover of all things beautiful, are untouched by lust and other filth. It is a sign of a divine decree calling you to wisdom, away from evil desires. Don't let yourself be attracted by false pleasures into going astray from this path. There is nothing more disgraceful and dangerous than such delinquent behavior. Embark on this learning and you will achieve the rest, believe me. It will cleanse and cultivate your soul, which before was in no way ready to receive the divine seed.

These books, which I am delighted to dedicate to you more than to have labored writing them, will abundantly instruct you, I think. To those eager to know and to behave, the course will teach the order demanded by everything that is, the lifestyle we, your dearest friends, endeavor to adopt, and the fruits of leisure. Become part, above all, of the very order I speak of, and be ever willing to choose the best.

5. As you know, even without the ailment that forced me to abandon professional teaching, I intended to retire so as to have time for philosophy. And so I came to the villa of our dearest friend Verecundus. What shall I say, with his permission? You well know him, how kind he is to all, but especially to me. There, we discussed all kinds of things, committing to writing those that might prove useful. This activity made me recover my health. As I was slowed down by the care to be precise in speaking, no disorder like immoderate quarreling crept into the debate. Also, by

nostrum litteris mandare placuisset, nec aliter dicendi necessitas nec labor recordationis esset. Agebant autem ista mecum Alypius et Navigius frater meus, et Licentius repente admirabiliter poeticae deditus. Trygetium item nobis militia reddiderat, qui tamquam veteranus adamavit historiam. Et iam in libris nonnihil habebamus.

CAPUT III
Occasio disputationis

6. Sed nocte quadam cum evigilassem de more mecumque ipse tacitus agitarem quae in mentem nescio unde veniebant (nam id mihi amore inveniendi veri iam in consuetudinem verterat, ita ut aut primam, si tales curae inerant, aut certe ultimam, dimidiam tamen fere noctis partem pervigil quodcumque cogitarem; nec me patiebar adolescentium lucubrationibus a meipso avocari, quia et illi per totum diem tantum agebant, ut nimium mihi videretur, si aliquid etiam noctium in studiorum laborem usurparent, et id a me ipsi quoque praeceptum habebant, ut aliquid et praeter codices secum agerent et apud sese habitare consuefacerent animum), ergo, ut dixi, vigilabam, cum ecce aquae sonus pone balneas quae praeterfluebat, eduxit me in aures, et animadversus est solito attentius. Mirum admodum mihi videbatur quod nunc clarius nunc pressius eadem aqua strepebat silicibus irruens. Coepi a me quaerere quaenam causa esset. Fateor, nihil occurrebat, cum Licentius lecto suo importunos percusso iuxta ligno sorices terruit seseque vigilantem hoc modo indicavit. Cui ego:

A. – Animadvertisti, inquam, Licenti (nam video tibi Musam tuam lumen ad lucubrandum accendisse), quomodo canalis iste inconstanter sonet?

L. – Iam, inquit, mihi hoc non est novum. Nam desiderio serenitatis cum expergefactus aliquando aurem admovissem, ne imber ingrueret, hoc agebat aqua ista quod nunc.

Approbavit Trygetius. Nam et ipse in eodem conclavi lecto suo cubans vigilabat, nobis nescientibus: erant enim tenebrae, quod in Italia etiam pecuniosis prope necesse est.

committing our production to writing, there would be no need either to repeat things or to make an undue effort of memory. With me were working Alypius, my brother Navigius and Licentius, who had suddenly discovered poetry. The army had given us back Trygetius, who as a veteran had fallen in love with history. We also had with us quite a number of books.

THREE
Whys and wherefores of the debate

6. Out of love for truth I had got into the habit of spending about half the night awake, thinking. For urgent matters it would be the earlier part, otherwise the latter. I had instructed the young men to extend their inquiry beyond the textbooks, and to get used to reflecting about such matters. I didn't want to distract myself with whatever they were doing at night. As they worked a lot during the day, it would have seemed excessive to expect them to go on working during the night. I was awake, as I said, when I could hear the sound of water just behind the bathrooms. On becoming aware, I paid more attention. What struck me was that the same water, on rushing against the stonework, produced an alternatively loud and soft sound. Much as I thought what the cause of it might be, I could not make out. Licentius, by banging on his bed to scare off some troublesome mice, indicated that he also was wide awake.

A. – I see that your Muse has lit the lamp for night work. Have you noticed the ups and downs of the sound of this water pipe?
L. – Yes, I have. As I like fair weather, when the sound woke me up I thought it was a sudden rainfall, but I realized it was this water.

Trygetius agreed. We didn't know that he too was awake, lying in bed in the same room. It was dark, an inconvenience which in Italy even the rich must put up with.

7. Ergo ubi vidi scholam nostram, quantacumque aderat, nam et Alypius et Navigius in urbem ierant, etiam illis horis non sopitam, et me cursus ille aquarum aliquid de se dicere admonebat:

A. – Quidnam vobis, inquam, videtur esse causae quod sic alternat hic sonus? Non enim quemquam putamus his horis vel transitu, vel re aliqua lavanda toties illum meatum interpellare.
L. – Quid putas, inquit Licentius, nisi alicubi folia cuiuscemodi quae autumno perpetuo copioseque decidunt, angustiis canalis intertrusa evinci aliquando atque cedere, ubi autem unda quae urgebat, pertransierit, rursum colligi atque stipari aut aliquid aliud vario casu foliorum natantium fieri, quod ad illum fluxum nunc refrenandum nunc emittendum similiter valeat?

Visum est mihi probabile aliud non habenti, confessusque sum, laudans ingenium eius, nihil me invenisse, cum diu quaesissem cur ita esset.

8. Tum interposito modico silentio:

A. – Merito, inquam, tu nihil mirabaris et apud Calliopam te intus tenebas.
L. – Merito, inquit ille, sed modo plane dedisti mihi magnum mirari.
A. – Quidnam hoc est?, inquam.
L. – Quod tu, inquit, ista miratus es.
A. – Unde enim solet, inquam, oboriri admiratio, aut quae huius vitii mater est, nisi res insolita praeter manifestum causarum ordinem?

Et ille:

L. – *Praeter manifestum*, inquit, accipio; nam praeter ordinem nihil mihi fieri videtur.

Hic ergo erectior spe alacriore quam soleo esse, cum aliquid ab his requiro, quod rem tantam et tam subito, heri pene ad ista conversus adolescentis animus concepisset, nulla unquam de his rebus inter nos antea quaestione agitata:
A. – Bene, inquam, bene; sed prorsus bene multum sensisti, multum ausus es. Hoc mihi crede; longo intervallo transcendis Heliconem, ad cuius verticem tamquam ad caelum pervenire conaris. Sed pervellem adesses huic sententiae, nam eam labefactare tentabo.

7. Alypius and Navigius had gone to town. I became aware that the rest of our class was not yet asleep even at such hours, and that the rushing of that water had called our attention.

A. – Why do you think this sound goes up and down in intensity? It is unlikely that someone, at this time of the night, steps into the gutter or washes something with such frequency.
L. – It is one of the two: either the many leaves that thickly fall in the autumn get stuck in some crack of the gutter to be dislodged by the mounting pressure, and get stuck again; or, a group of floating leaves gather together and temporarily block the flow of water, which on being released causes the same effect.

It looked likely to me, who had no better explanation to offer. I praised his brains, confessing that nothing had occurred to me despite the time spent thinking.

8. We paused, then:

A. – That's why you did not wonder; your poetry kept you entertained.
L. – True enough, but I greatly wonder at you now.
A. – How come?
L. – That you marvel at such things.
A. – And where does the sense of wonder come from? Isn't the origin of this vice something unusual outside the obvious order of things?
L. Outside the *obvious* order, yes; not outside order as such. Nothing is to be found outside it.

Here I was startled more than I usually was when asking them such questions. A mere teenager, introduced only yesterday to such matters, had suddenly found the right answer to a question never before brought to our attention.
A. – Well, well, you dared much, and understood even more. Believe me, your spirit has soared higher than Mount Helicon. Its heavenly summit is within your reach. Now stick to your position, for I will try to attack it.

L. – Sine, inquit, modo me mihi, quaeso te; nam valde in aliud intendi animum.

Hic ergo nonnihil metuens ne studio poeticae penitus provolutus a philosophia longe raperetur:

A. – Irritor, inquam, abs te versus istos tuos omni metrorum genere cantando et ululando insectari, qui inter te atque veritatem immaniorem murum quam inter amantes tuos conantur erigere; nam in se illi vel inolita rimula respirabant. Pyramum enim ille tum canere instituerat.

9. Quod cum severiore quam putabat voce dixissem, subtacuit aliquantum. Et ego iam reliqueram coepta et ad me redieram, ne frustra occupare praeoccupatum atque inepte vellem. Tum ille:

L. – "*Egomet meo indicio miser quasi sorex*" [Terence, *Eunuchus* 1024], inquit, non dictum est commodius apud Terentium quam nunc dici a me de me potest. Sed sane illud ultimum fortasse in contrarium vertetur: quod enim ait ille: "*Hodie perii,*" ego hodie forte inveniar. Nam si non contemnitis quod superstitiosi solent etiam de muribus augurari, si ego illum murem, vel soricem, qui me tibi vigilantem detulit, strepitu meo commonui, si quid sapit redire in cubile suum secumque conquiescere, cur non ego ipse isto strepitu vocis tuae commonear philosophari potius quam cantare? Nam illa est, ut tibi quotidie probanti iam coepi credere, vera et inconcussa nostra habitatio. Quare si tibi molestum non est atque fieri debere arbitraris, roga quod vis: defendam, quantum possum, ordinem rerum nihilque praeter ordinem fieri posse asseram. Tantum enim eum animo imbibi atque hausi, ut etiamsi me quisquam in hac disputatione superarit, etiam hoc nulli temeritati, sed rerum ordini tribuam. Neque enim res ipsa, sed Licentius superabitur.

CAPUT IV
Nihil omnino sine causa fieri

10. Ego rursum gaudens eis me restitui. Tum Trygetio:

A. – Quid, inquam, tibi videtur?

T. – Faveo quidem, inquit, ordini plurimum, sed incertus sum tamen et rem tantam diligentissime discuti cupio.

L. – Please leave me alone now; I have other things to think about.

Here I somewhat feared that he might wholly stray from philosophy by his poetry.

A. – I feel sorry for your singing and howling these verses of yours in all kinds of rhythms. They are erecting a wall, between you and the truth of things, thicker and more impenetrable than the one that divided the lovers Pyramus and Thisbe you are crooning about. At least they could whisper to each other through a crack.

9. As I had used a harsher tone than he expected, he kept quiet for a while. So did I and recovered my poise. It would have been useless and tactless to distract him from his worries. But he said:

L. – I can apply to myself Terentius's verse "*I have got myself into worse misery than a mouse*" more appropriately than he applied it to his character. Not his conclusion though, which can be turned inside out. What he deems lost by his "*today I perish*," I will perhaps find today. If you agree that soothsayers can divine from mice, it was one of these rodents that betrayed to you my being awake. As my banging urged it into scampering off back into its hole, why should I not attribute to this same banging the raising of your voice urging me to philosophize instead of play? I have begun to accept your daily proofs. Philosophy is indeed our true and unshaken abode. If you don't mind then, and you think you should, ask what you wish: I will defend the order of things insofar as I can, asserting that nothing is outside it. It has sunk so deeply into me, that even in the event of my being defeated in the debate, I will not attribute my defeat to chance, but to that very order of things. I, Licentius, will be defeated, not truth.

FOUR
Nothing happens without a cause

10. Happy again, I went back to them. I asked Trygetius,

A. – What do you think?

T. – Mostly I am in favor of order, but uncertain. I am eager to discuss such a weighty matter in depth, however.

A. – Favorem, inquam, tuum illa ergo pars habeat: nam quod incertus es, etiam cum Licentio ac meipso tibi puto esse commune.
L. – Prorsus, ait Licentius, ego huius sententiae certus sum. Quid enim dubitem parietem, cuius mentionem fecisti, antequam plane se erexerit, diruere? Non enim vere poetica tantum me avertere a philosophia potest quantum inveniendi veri diffidentia.

Tum Trygetius gaudentibus verbis:
T. – Habemus, inquit, iam quod plus est, Licentium non Academicum; eos enim ille studiosissime defendere solebat.
L. – Haec modo, inquit, omitte, quaeso, ne me hoc vafrum quiddam et captatorium a nescio qua divina re, quae mihi ostentare se coepit et cui me inhiantem suspendo, detorqueat atque disrumpat.

Hic ego multo uberius cernens abundare laetitias meas quam vel optare aliquando ausus sum, versum istum gestiens effudi:
A. – *"Sic Pater ille deum faciat, sic altus Apollo"* [Terence, *Eunuchus* 1024] incipias: perducet enim ipse, si sequimur quo nos ire iubet atque ubi ponere sedem, qui dat modo augurium nostrisque illabitur animis. Nec enim *altus Apollo* est, qui in speluncis, in montibus, in nemoribus, nidore thuris pecudumque calamitate concitatus implet insanos, sed alius profecto est, alius ille altus veridicus, atque ipsa (quid enim verbis ambiam?) Veritas: cuius vates sunt quicumque possunt esse sapientes. Ergo aggrediamur, Licenti, freti pietate cultores, et vestigiis nostris ignem perniciosum fumosarum cupiditatum opprimamus.

11. - Iam, inquit, interroga, oro te, si possim hoc tantum nescio quid explicare, et tuis verbis et meis.

A. – Hoc ipsum, inquam, mihi responde, primo unde tibi videatur aqua ista non temere sic sed ordine influere. Nam quod illa ligneolis canalibus superlabitur et ducitur usque in usus nostros, potest ad ordinem pertinere. Factum est enim ab hominibus ratione utentibus, ut uno eius itinere simul et biberent et lavarent et pro locorum opportunitatibus consequens erat ut ita fieret. Quod vero illa, ut dicis, folia sic inciderunt, ut hoc quod admirati sumus eveniret, quo tandem rerum ordine ac non potius casu factum putabimus?
L. – Quasi vero, inquit ille, aliter atque ceciderunt debuisse aut potuisse cadere cuiquam videri potest, serenissime intuenti nihil

A. – Let Licentius's party enjoy your support. As for your uncertainty, both Licentius and I will share it with you.
L. – I am absolutely certain of what I said. What should make me hesitate in knocking down the wall you were talking about, before it gets fully built? Not poetry, for sure; but rather despair of finding truth.
T. (gleefully) – Hear, hear. Licentius has parted company with the Academicians, whom he used to praise so zealously.
L. – Don't mention that, please. Their crafty and cunning doctrines threaten to distract me and to shatter this divine reality I have glimpsed, which has me yearning with desire.

Here, seeing that I was getting happier than I could have possibly desired or dared, I blurted out this verse:
A. – "*May sovereign and fatherly Apollo fashion a god.*" Start with this, and He who now gives but hints to our minds will lead us to where we are meant to fix our abode. Aren't there two sovereign Apollos? One dwells in caves, on mountains, in forests, in the smell of incense and of cattle, violently causing madness. The other, no less true and no less sovereign is, not to mince words, Truth itself, whose prophets are those who can be wise. Therefore, Licentius, let us rely on piety and be on our way. We shall extinguish the dangerous fire of stifling desires under our stomping feet.

11. **L.** – Now ask me, please. Maybe I will be able to explain this great thing, whatever it is, in words common to both of us.

A. – Answer this first. Why do you think this water flows in an orderly and not in a disorderly fashion? I grant that its flowing in wooden conduits to where we need it, belongs to order. But this is a man-made order, for the sake of those who want to drink or to wash, and by constructing one single conduit they can do both. But those leaves that fell, as you said, causing us to wonder, why on earth should they have done so because of order and not rather because of chance?
L. – He who most clearly understands that nothing happens without a cause will not admit of a different reason for their falling.

posse fieri sine causa. Quid iam vis persequar? Situs arborum atque ramorum, ipsumque pondus quantum natura foliis imposuit? Quid, aeris vel mobilitatem qua volitant, vel mollitiem qua descendunt, variosque lapsus pro affectione caeli, pro onere, pro figuris suis, caeterisque innumerabilibus atque obscurioribus causis , quid me attinet quaerere? Latent ista sensus nostros, penitus latent: illud tamen quod aggressae quaestioni satis est, nescio quomodo animum non latet, nihil fieri sine causa. Potest enim odiosus percontator pergere quaerere: quae causa erat ut ibi arbores ponerentur? Respondebo secutos esse homines uber terrae.
A. – Quid si fructuosae arbores non sunt ac temere natae sunt?
L. – Et hic respondebo nos parum videre; nam temerariam, quae illas genuit, nequaquam esse naturam. Quid plura? Aut aliquid sine causa fieri doceat aut nihil fieri nisi certo causarum ordine credite.

CAPUT V
Ordine cuncta Deus administrat

12. A. – Cui ego: Licet, inquam, me odiosum percontatorem voces (vix enim possum non esse, qui expugnavi ne cum Pyramo et Thysbe colloquereris) pergam tamen quaerere abs te. Natura ista quam vis videri ordinatam, cui bono, ut de caeteris rebus innumerabilibus taceam, istas ipsas arbores quae fructus non afferunt, procreavit?

At illo cogitante quid diceret, ait Trygetius:
T. – Numquidnam usus arbustorum in solis fructibus praebetur hominibus? Quanta sunt alia, quae umbra, quae lignis, postremo quae ipsis frondibus seu foliis fiant?
L. – Noli obsecro, inquit ille, interrogationibus eius haec reddere. Innumerabilia sunt enim quae proferri possunt, ex quibus nulla est hominibus utilitas, aut certe ita latet vel imbecilla est, ut ab hominibus, praesertim nobis, erui defendive non possit. Ipse potius nos doceat, quomodo aliquid fiat quod non causa praecesserit.
A. – Post, inquam, ista videbimus. Non enim iam me necesse est esse doctorem, cum tu qui iam tantae rei te certum esse professus es, adhuc me nihil docueris nimium discere cupientem et propter hoc solum dies noctesque vigilantem.

What do you want me to investigate? The location of the trees, their branches, and the weight of leaf that nature imposes on each branch? Or the motion of the air in which the leaves flutter, or its viscosity acting against their coming down, or their intermittent falling due to the weather, their weight, their shape and countless even more obscure causes that I should be concerned with? All these are utterly hidden to our senses. What is enough to answer the question, although I don't know why it is not hidden from the mind, is that nothing happens without a cause. An irksome busybody could go on asking why the trees grew where they did. I would reply that people planted them there because the soil was fertile. And what if the trees failed to bear fruit, or grew there by accident? To such I would answer that it is we who see little; but that nature, which brought them forth, does not act helter-skelter. What else? Either you succeed in convincing me that something can happen without a cause, or you accept that nothing happens without a definite hierarchy of causes.

FIVE
God governs everything in order

12. A. – You call me an irksome busybody. So be it, for I deserve the epithet for wrenching you out of talking with Pyramus and Thisbe. I shall go on asking then. To whose benefit did this ordered nature of yours bring forth sterile trees, not to speak of countless other things?

As Licentius was thinking what to say, Trygetius intervened.

T. – Is fruit production the only use of plants? What about shade, timber, and, lastly, leafy branches?

L. – Don't answer like that, please. There are indeed countless things with no apparent usefulness we could talk about. Their utility is either so hidden or it amounts to so little that it is impossible for us to perceive or to assert. Let Augustine rather explain to us how anything might happen without a previous cause.

A. – Later. There is no need for me to teach any more, for you, who have declared yourself so certain on such heady matter, can teach me nothing more than this. I have spent days and nights on this topic, really wishing to learn.

13. L. – Quo me mittis?, inquit. An quia levius te sequor quam illa folia ventos, quibus in profluentem aquam iaciuntur, ut eis cadere parum sit nisi etiam trahantur? Nam quid aliud erit cum Licentius et Augustinum et ea quae sunt in media philosophia docet?
A. – Noli obsecro, inquam, aut te tantum abiicere aut me extollere. Nam et ego in philosophia puer sum et non nimis curo, cum interrogo, per quem mihi ille respondeat, qui me quotidie querulum accipit: cuius te quidem credo quandoque vatem futurum; neque hoc *quandoque* forsitan longum est. Sed tamen alii quoque multum sepositi ab huiusmodi studiis docere aliquid possunt, cum disserentium societati quasi vinculis interrogationum coarctantur. Idem autem aliquid non est nihil. An non vides (tuo enim simili utar libentius) illa ipsa folia quae feruntur ventis, quae undis innatant, resistere aliquantum praecipitanti se flumini et de rerum ordine homines commonere, si tamen hoc quod abs te defenditur verum est?

14. Hic ille lecto etiam exsiliens prae laetitia:

L. – Quis neget, Deus magne, inquit, te cuncta ordine administrare? Quam se omnia tenent! Quam ratis successionibus in nodos suos urgentur! Quanta et quam multa facta sunt ut haec loqueremur! Quanta fiunt ut te inveniamus! Unde enim hoc ipsum, nisi ex rerum ordine manat et ducitur, quod evigilavimus, quod illum sonum advertisti, quod quaesisti tecum causam, quod tu causam tantillae rei non invenisti? Sorex etiam prodit, ut ego vigilans prodar. Postremo tuus etiam ipse sermo, te fortasse id non agente (non enim cuiquam in potestate est quid veniat in mentem), sic nescio quomodo circumagitur ut me ipse doceat quid tibi debeam respondere.

Namque, oro te, si haec a nobis dicta sunt, litteris, ut instituisti, mandata pervagentur paulo latius ad hominum famam, nonne ita res magna videbitur ut de illa consultus aliquis vates magnus aut Chaldaeus respondere debuerit, multo antequam evenit? Quod si respondisset, ita divinus diceretur, ita efferretur laudibus omnium, ut tamen ex eo nemo quaerere auderet cur folium ab arbore ceciderit aut utrum mus oberrans iacenti homini molestus fuerit? Numquidnam enim talia futura quisquam illorum aut per

13. L. – What are you getting me into? Am I not following you like these leaves follow the wind that makes them fall into the running water? For them, to fall and to be dragged along is one and the same thing. How could it be now that Licentius teaches Augustine such things as make up the core of philosophy?
A. – Don't demean yourself or extol me, please. Even I am a boy when it comes to philosophy. When in the quest for something, I don't care very much through whom He gives answers to my daily, longing search. You yourself will perhaps be one of his priests one day, maybe sooner than you think. Even outsiders to these studies can teach something, by asking questions which force those who know into answering. It is something. To use your own words, don't you see how those leaves driven by the wind, or floating over water, oppose some resistance to the forces acting upon them? In so doing they teach something to men, if what you assert is true.

14. Licentius jumped out of bed in excitement.

L. – Great God! Who can deny that You are the orderly ruler of all? Everything is related to everything else, each thing impelled to its appointed effects by a series of fixed laws. They are so many and act in so many fashions as to force us to speak of them endlessly. In so doing, we find You. What indeed but this same order caused and directed all this, namely our being awake, your paying attention to that strange noise, your asking yourself questions, your not finding the cause of such a trifle? And it was a mouse that betrayed my being awake to you. Lastly, you may not have thought enough about what you said, for no one can control all the ideas that come to mind. But your very words, I don't know how, suggest to me what I should answer to you now. Tell me: suppose that, as you suggested, we committed to writing these things we are talking about, and broadcast them to a wide audience. If a great soothsayer, a Chaldean for instance, foretold our writing and its spreading before it happened, wouldn't that be truly wonderful? In such a case people would praise him to the skies, and no one would dare ask him about falling leaves and rummaging mice that get people out of bed. Has any of them, however, foretold any such thing either on his

se dixit aliquando, aut a consultore coactus est dicere? Atqui, si futurum quemdam librum non ignobilem diceret et id necessario eventurum videret (non enim posset aliter divinare) profecto quidquid volitatio foliorum in agro, quidquid vilissima bestiola in domo facit, tam sunt in rerum ordine necessaria quam illae litterae. His enim verbis fiunt, quae sine illis praecedentibus vilissimis rebus nec in mente venire possent, nec ore procedere posterisque mandari. Quare iam, rogo, nemo ex me quaerat cur quidque fiat. Satis est nihil fieri, nihil gigni quod non aliqua causa genuerit ac moverit.

CAPUT VI
Ordo omnia complectitur

15. A. – Hic apparet te, inquam, nescire, adolescens, quam multa et a qualibus viris contra divinationem dicta sint. Sed responde nunc, non utrum fiat aliquid sine causa (nam id iam video te nolle respondere) sed ordo iste susceptus tuus bonumne quidquam an malum tibi esse videatur.

Et ille submurmurans:

L. – Non, inquit, sic rogasti, ut unum e duobus queam respondere. Video hic enim quamdam medietatem. Nam ordo mihi nec bonum nec malum videtur.

A. – Quid saltem censes, inquam, ordini esse contrarium?

L. – Nihil, ait ille. Nam quomodo esse contrarium quidquam potest ei rei quae totum occupavit, totum obtinuit? Quod enim erit ordini contrarium, necesse erit esse praeter ordinem. Nihil autem esse praeter ordinem video. Nihil igitur ordini oportet putare esse contrarium.

T. – Ergone, ait Trygetius, contrarius ordini error non est?

L. – Nullo modo, inquit. Nam neminem video errare sine causa. Causarum autem series ordine includitur. Et error ipse non solum gignitur causa, sed etiam gignit aliquid cui causa sit. Quamobrem quo extra ordinem non est, eo non potest ordini esse contrarius.

16. Et cum tacuisset Trygetius egoque meipsum non caperem gaudio, quod videbam adolescentem carissimi amici filium etiam

own initiative or forced by somebody's asking? Successfully foretelling the publishing of a great book as something necessary, for that is what divination is, would make things like the fluttering of leaves and the insignificant patter of house-mice as necessary as the written book. Everything would belong to the same order. In fact, without the insignificant things that happened before, what we are saying would not have even occurred to our minds, let alone our conversing about them or preserving them for posterity. Therefore, please, let no one ask me why anything happens. It is enough to know that nothing happens without an efficient cause nor comes to be without a generating one.

SIX
Order encompasses everything

15. A. – It would appear that you are too young to be aware of which authorities have condemned divination and how much. Now tell me not so much whether anything can happen without a cause, for I see you have no intention of tackling that; but whether this order of yours appears to you as a good or a bad thing.
L. – You didn't frame the question so as to leave me one of two choices. I see a middle course here, namely that order seems to me neither good nor bad.
A. – At any rate, what do you think might be contrary to order?
L. – Nothing. How can anything be contrary to a whole encompassing everything? Anything contrary to order, strictly speaking, ought to be outside it. But I see nothing outside order, therefore there must be nothing contrary to it.
T. – Ah, but isn't error contrary to order?
L. – Not at all. I cannot see anyone making a mistake without a cause. Any series of causes must be included in order. Even error as such is not only due to a cause, but itself becomes the cause of something else as well. Then what is not outside order cannot be contrary to it

16. This silenced Trygetius, while I could scarcely contain myself for joy. Here was a teenager, son of a dear friend of mine, whom

meum fieri, nec solum, verum in amicum quoque iam mihi surgere atque grandescere, et cuius studium vel in mediocres litteras desperaveram, quasi respecta possessione sua toto impetu in mediam venire philosophiam. Quod dum tacitus miror et exaestuo in gratulatione, subito ille quasi mente quadam correptus exclamat:
L. – O si possem dicere quod volo! Rogo, ubiubi estis, verba, succurrite. Et bona et mala in ordine sunt. Credite, si vultis, nam quomodo id explicem nescio.

CAPUT VII
Deus non diligit mala licet ad ordinem pertineant

17. Ego mirabar et tacebam. Trygetius autem ubi vidit hominem paululum quasi digesta ebrietate affabilem factum redditumque colloquio:

T. – Absurdum, inquit, mihi videtur, Licenti, et plane alienum a veritate quod dicis; sed quaeso patiare me paululum, nec perturbes clamitando.
L. – Dic quod vis, ait ille: non enim metuo ne me auferas ab eo quod video ac pene teneo.
T. – Utinam, inquit, ab eo quem defendis ordine devius non sis, non tanta in Deum feraris (ut mitius loquar) incuria. Quid enim potuit dici magis impium, quam etiam mala ordine contineri? Certe enim Deus amat ordinem.
L. – Vere amat, ait ille; ab ipso manat et cum ipso est. Et si quid potest de re tantum alta convenientius dici, cogita, quaeso, ipse tecum. Nec enim sum idoneus qui te ista nunc doceam.
T. – Quid cogitem?, inquit Trygetius. Accipio prorsus quod dicis satisque mihi est in eo quod intelligo. Certe enim et mala dixisti ordine contineri et ipsum ordinem manare a summo Deo atque ab eo diligi. Ex quo sequitur ut et mala sint a summo Deo et mala Deus diligat.

18. In qua conclusione timui Licentio. At ille ingemiscens difficultate verborum nec omnino quaerens quid responderet, sed quemadmodum quod respondendum erat promeret:

I treated as if he were my own son. A strong bond of friendship was also developing between the two of us, for after despairing of his education, all of a sudden he had burst into the very core of philosophy as if he owned it. As I silently bubbled over in thanksgiving, he said in a kind of rapture:
L. – Would that I were able to say what I want! Words, wherever you are, come and help. And you two believe me if you wish, for I am at a loss to explain.

SEVEN
God does not love evil things even if they belong to order

17. In amazement I said nothing. Trygetius waited until the other cooled down and became approachable again.

T. – What you said, Licentius, seems to me both absurd and quite false. Please be a little patient and don't confuse me with your shouting.
L. – As you wish, for I have no fear of your distracting me from what I see and almost hold in my hands.
T. – Would that you neither went astray from the order you defend, nor, to put it mildly, that you should be enticed into neglect of God. What is more impious than saying that evil is part of order? Surely God loves order.
L. – He truly does. It proceeds from Him and is to be found in Him. If anything better can be said of such a lofty matter, think of it yourself. I am not up to teaching it to you.
T. – Me think? I stick to your words, if I understand you. You said that good and evil equally belong to order, and that order comes from God who loves it. Therefore evil comes from God who loves it.

18. This conclusion made me fear for Licentius. He was groping for words, not so much as to what to say, but how to put it as the matter deserved.

L. – Non diligit Deus mala, inquit; nec ob aliud, nisi quia ordinis non est ut Deus mala diligat. Et ordinem ideo multum diligit, quia per eum non diligit mala. At vero ipsa mala qui possunt non esse in ordine, cum Deus illa non diligat? Nam iste ipse est malorum ordo ut non diligantur a Deo. An parvus rerum ordo tibi videtur, ut et bona Deus diligat et non diligat mala? Ita nec praeter ordinem sunt mala, quae non diligit Deus, et ipsum tamen ordinem diligit: hoc ipsum enim diligit diligere bona, et non diligere mala, quod est magni ordinis, et divinae dispositionis. Qui ordo atque dispositio, quia universitatis congruentiam ipsa distinctione custodit, fit ut mala etiam esse necesse sit. Ita quasi ex antithesis quodammodo, quod nobis etiam in oratione iucundum est, id est ex contrariis, omnium simul rerum pulchritudo figuratur.

19. Post hoc intersiluit modice. Et repente sese erigens qua Trygetius lectum habebat:

L. – Nam quaero ex te, quaeso, inquit, iustusne sit Deus?

Tacebat ille, nimis, ut postea retulit, admirans et horrens subito condiscipuli et familiaris sui afflatum nova inspiratione sermonem. Quo tacente, ille ita secutus est:

L. – Si enim Deus iustum non esse responderis, tu videris quid agas, qui me dudum impietatis arguebas. Si autem, ut nobis traditur, nosque ipsius ordinis necessitate sentimus, iustus est Deus, sua cuique distribuendo utique iustus est. Quae autem distributio dici potest, ubi distinctio nulla est? Aut quae distinctio, si bona sunt omnia? Quidve praeter ordinem reperiri potest, si Dei iustitia bonorum malorumque meritis sua cuique redduntur? Iustum autem Deum omnes fatemur. Totum igitur ordine includitur.

Quibus dictis resilit e strato, et iam lenior voce, cum ei verbum nemo faceret:

L. – Nihilne mihi, inquit, vel tu qui compulisti ad ista, respondes?

20. Cui ego:

A. – Nova nunc religio isthaec in te incessit cedo, inquam. Sed quod videbitur, per diem respondebo, qui mihi iam videtur redire nisi lunae est ille qui fenestris fulgor inducitur. Simul et tacendum

L. – God does not love evil. It would not be in order for Him to do so. He loves order so much that for its sake He does not love evil. Since God does not love evil, does it mean that there can be any evil outside order? This is precisely the order of evil things, that God should not love them. Do you think it is a mean order that God should love good things and not evil ones? Evil things are not outside order because God does not love them. He in fact loves to love good things, and also loves not to love evil things. This is the greater order of divine disposition. Both order and disposition keep the universe together by this very distinction, rendering the existence of evil somewhat necessary. This clashing of contraries, which we love so much in rhetoric, gives body to the overall beauty of the universe.

19. There was some silence. Then suddenly, standing over Trygetius's bed, he blurted out:

L. – Tell me now, I ask, is God just?

Trygetius kept quiet. As he later recalled, he was at once astonished and frightened at this sudden burst of inspiration by his fellow learner and friend. Seeing him still silent, Licentius went on:

L. – If you answer that God is not just, it is your business, and so much for your accusing me of impiety a short while ago. But tradition, as well as the need for order, we all feel, tell us that He is just, and that He gives to each what is due. Could there be any distribution without distinction? Or any distinction, if things were all equally good? Can anything be apart from order, if by God's justice both good and evil are given their due? We all admit God to be just. Therefore order encompasses everything.

Having so spoken he fell back into bed. As no one was answering back, he lowered his tone and asked me:

L. – You got me into all this. Have you nothing to say?

20. A. – I grant that you have begun to understand anew. It appears that I shall have to answer in daytime, for I notice the light of dawn through the windows, unless it be the moon. Now we must see to it that none of the good things you have said, Licentius, is forgotten. Our literary undertaking has always been

est ne tanta bona tua, Licenti, absorbeat oblivio. Quando enim nostrae litterae non sibi haec mandari flagitent? Dicam plane tibi quod sentio, disputabo adversum te quantum possum; non enim mihi, si me viceris, maior triumphus dari potest. Si autem vel calliditati vel acuto cuidam errori hominum, quorum partes suscipere tentabo, cesserit imbecillitas tua, quae minus pasta eruditione disciplinarum tantum Deum fortasse sustinere non poterit, res te ipsa commonebit quantae tibi vires, ut in eum firmior redeas, parandae sint: simul quia et istam disputationem nostram elimatius volo provenire; non enim eam grossis auribus debeo.

Nam Zenobius noster multa mecum saepe de rerum ordine contulit, cui alta percontanti nunquam satisfacere potui, seu propter obscuritatem rerum, seu propter temporum angustias. Crebrarum autem ille procrastinationum usque adeo impatiens fuit, ut me, quo diligentius et copiosius respondere cogerer, etiam carmine provocaret, et bono carmine, unde illum magis ames. Sed neque tunc tibi legi potuit ab istarum rerum studio remotissimo, neque nunc potest. Nam profectio eius tam repentina et perturbata fuit tumultu illo, ut nihil istorum venire nobis in mentem potuerit; nam id relinquere mihi responsuro statuerat et multa concurrunt cur ei sermo iste mittatur. Primum est, quia debetur; deinde, quia cuiusmodi nunc vitam ducamus, etiam sic indicari eius in nos benevolentiae decet; postremo, quod in gaudio de spe tua nemini cedit. Nam et cum praesens esset, pro familiaritate patris tui vel potius omnium nostrum, multum sollicitus erat ne ingenii tui quaedam scintillae, quas diligenter animadvertebat, non tam conflarentur cura mea quam tua exstinguerentur incuria. Et cum te poeticae quoque studiosum esse cognoverit, sic gratulabitur, ut eum mihi gestientem videre iam videar.

CAPUT VIII

Licentius philosophiae amore succensus. A Monnica reprehenditur. Liberalium disciplinarum utilitas.

21. L. – Nihil mihi quidem gratius facies, inquit; sed sive mobilitatem meam et puerilem levitatem ridebitis, sive aliquo vere divino nutu et ordine fit in nobis, non vobis dubitem dicere: pigrior

that we put everything in writing. Let me speak my mind. I will debate against you with all my might. If you defeat me, I could not conceive of a better triumph for myself. I may succeed, though, in exposing your weakness with the cunning and sophistries of famous men, whose part I will play. Without the strong food of good instruction you will perhaps fail to defend the cause of so great a God. This will warn you of how much strength you are in need of on your way to Him, and how much I intend this debate of ours to succeed. I want to polish it to the standard of a fine audience.

Our friend Zenobius and I often met over this matter of order. He raised questions way above my capacity to answer, either because they were really hard or because of lack of time. He became so impatient over my frequent delays that he tried to coax me into answering more and better with a poem he wrote. It is a good one, so that you may love him the more for it. It was not for your reading then, remote as you were from intellectually tackling such matters, and it is not for your reading now. He left in such hurry and distress, because of the disturbances in Milan, that none of these things could possibly come to our minds. He had decided to leave me with a copy so that I could reply to him, and many things have happened that force me to write to him. First, it is a duty. Second, it is a good thing to inform him of our present lifestyle in gratitude for his being so good to us. Lastly, no one gainsays him in the hope he has in you. When he was here he cared a lot that the spark of genius he had noted in you should neither flare up because of my fanning it nor be put out because of your negligence. On knowing of your recently acquired taste for poetry he will be so happy that I can see him exult with joy.

EIGHT

Licentius falls in love with philosophy. Enter Monica. The liberal arts.

21. L. You couldn't have done me a better turn. Whether it is a typical boyish fickle change of heart at which you may laugh, or something truly induced by a divine command, let me tell you: I

sum ad illa metra subito effectus; alia, longe alia nescio quid mihi nunc luce resplenduit. Pulchrior est philosophia, fateor, quam Thisbe, quam Pyramus, quam illa Venus et Cupido talesque omnimodi amores.

Et cum suspirio gratias Christo agebat. Accepi ego haec, quid dicam, libenter: aut quid non dicam? Accipiat quisque ut volet, nihil curo, nisi quod forte immodice gaudebam.

22. Interea post paululum dies sese aperuit. Surrexerunt illi, et ego illacrymans multa oravi, cum audio Licentium succinentem illud Propheticum laete atque garrule:
L. – "*Deus virtutum, converte nos, et ostende faciem tuam, et salvi erimus*" [Ps 79:8].

Quod pridie post coenam cum ad requisita naturae foras exisset, paulo clarius cecinit, quam ut mater nostra ferre posset, quod illo loco talia continuo repetita canerentur. Nihil enim aliud dicebat, quoniam ipsum cantilenae modum nuper hauserat et amabat, ut fit, melos inusitatum. Obiurgavit eum religiosissima, ut scis, femina, ob hoc ipsum quod inconveniens locus cantico esset. Tunc ille dixerat, iocans:
L. – Quasi vero si quis hic me inimicus includeret, non erat Deus auditurus vocem meam?

23. Ergo mane cum regressus esset solus (nam uterque ob eamdem causam processerat) accessit ad lectulum meum.

L. – Verum dic mihi, inquit, ita fiat nobis quod vis, quid me existimes.

Atque ego adolescentis dexteram apprehendens:
A. – Quid, inquam, existimem sentis, credis, intellegis. Neque enim arbitror te frustra heri tamdiu cecinisse ut virtutum Deus converso tibi se ostendat.

At ille cum admiratione recordatus:
L. – Magnum, inquit, dicis et verum. Non enim meipsum parum movet quod modo tam aegre avocabar a nugis illis carminis mei et iam redire ad eas piget et pudet, ita totus in quaedam magna et mira subvehor. Nonne hoc est vere in Deum converti? Simul et

have suddenly lost interest in all this poetry. An indescribable light now shines within me. I swear that philosophy is much more attractive than Pyramus, Thisbe, Venus, and Cupid, and such like amorous stories.

Then he sighed and gave thanks to Christ. I was delighted to hear all that; why deny it? I don't care about whatever anyone may say, except perhaps that I may have exceeded due measure in my rejoicing.

22. Shortly afterward daylight broke. They got up, and I shed tears while praying. Whereupon I heard happy Licentius singing rather noisily a verse from Psalm 79:

"*O God of hosts, convert us. Show us your face and we shall be saved.*"

The previous day, after dinner, he had gone out for a call of nature singing this same hymn. It was a little louder than my mother could stand, for she suddenly heard it again and again issuing from that place. He was getting repetitious, for he had recently learned it, and rather liked the new tune. That most pious woman scolded him precisely for singing it in such an unbecoming place. But he joked:

L. – So what? If an enemy were to lock me in here, wouldn't God hear my voice?

23. In the morning, the two friends went out for the same reason. Licentius came back alone and approached my bed.

L. – Tell me the truth, whatever may happen between us. What do you think of me?

I took his right hand and replied:

A. – You already sense, believe, and understand what I think of you. I do not think that yesterday you sang so long in vain. The God of hosts paid attention to your addressing Him.

He recalled with a start:

L. – True indeed! I am shocked to think that it was such a little while ago that I found it so painful to be diverted from my little songs. Right now I feel disgust and shame at the very thought of returning to them. I am being carried away by things great and wonderful. Is

illud gaudeo, quod frustra mihi scrupulus superstitionis iniectus est quod tali loco talia cantitabam.
A. – Mihi, inquam, neque hoc displicet, et ad illum ordinem puto pertinere ut etiam hinc aliquid diceremus. Nam illi cantico et locum ipsum quo illa offensa est et noctem congruere video. A quibus enim rebus putas nos orare ut convertamur ad Deum eiusque faciem videamus, nisi a quodam coeno corporis atque sordibus et item a tenebris quibus nos error involvit? Aut quid est aliud converti, nisi ab immoderatione vitiorum, virtute ac temperantia in sese attolli? Quidve aliud est Dei facies, quam ipsa cui suspiramus et cui nos amatae mundos pulchrosque reddimus, veritas?
L. – Melius dici non potest, inquit exclamans. (Deinde suppressius quasi ad aurem): Vide, quaeso, quanta occurrerunt, ut credam erga nos aliquid prosperiore ordine fieri.

24. A. – Si ordinem, inquam, curas, redeundum tibi est ad illos versus. Nam eruditio disciplinarum liberalium, modesta sane ac succincta, et alacriores et perseverantiores et comptiores exhibet amatores amplectendae veritati, ut et ardentius appetant, et constantius insequantur et inhaereant postremo dulcius, quae vocatur, Licenti, beata vita. Qua nominata, omnes sese erigunt, et quasi attendunt in manus, utrum habeas quod dare possis egentibus variisque morbis impeditis. Quibus sapientia cum praecipere coeperit ut medicum perferant seque cum aliqua patientia curari sinant, in pannos suos recidunt. Quorum concalefactione tabificati, scabiem voluptatum aerumnosarum scalpunt libentius, quam ut monita medici paululum dura et morbis onerosa perpetiendo atque subeundo valetudini sanorum lucique reddantur. Itaque illo summi Dei nomine ac sensu tamquam stipe contenti vivunt miseri, vivunt tamen. Alios autem viros, vel, ut verius loquamur, alias animas, dum hoc corpus agunt, iam thalamo suo digna coniux ille optimus ac pulcherrimus quaerit, quibus non vivere, sed beate vivere satis sit. Vade ergo interim ad illas Musas. Verumtamen, scis quid te facere velim?
L. – Iube, ait, quod placet.
A. – Ubi se, inquam, Pyramus et illa eius super invicem, ut cantaturus es, interemerint, in dolore ipso, quo tuum carmen vehementius inflammari decet, habes commodissimam opportunitatem. Arripe

that not to be truly converted to God? I am also happy to have got rid of the superstition that it is bad to sing in that place.
A. – So am I, for I am pleased to relate all this to that same order, and to continue speaking about it. I see a connection between the singing, the place, the night, and my mother's taking offense at it. When we pray to convert to God and to see His face, don't we ask to be liberated from bodily and other filth, and from the darkness of error? What else is to be converted, than going from immoderate vice to accepting virtue and temperance? Is not God's face that very truth we yearn for, and to which we show our love by being clean and beautiful?
L. (raising his voice) – You couldn't have said it better. (Then whispering into A.'s ear): See how many things happened? They make me think that something great is in store for us.

24. A. – If you care about order, you should go back to those verses. Instruction in the liberal arts, in moderation and to the point, produces lively, persevering, and refined lovers of truth. Their aim is ardently to desire, constantly to pursue, and eventually lovingly cling to what is called, Licentius, the happy life. Mention happiness, and all stand up, hands extended, to beg of you some alms as if they were poor wretches in the grip of disease. But as wisdom begins to demand that they take themselves to the physician and let themselves be cured by him, they return to their rags. Wasting away in the warmth of their rags, they scratch the itchy scabs of troublesome lust rather than submit to the physician's prescriptions. These are hard at first, but effective against the disorder, so that with a little endurance and submission they would be restored to health and to the light of understanding. But instead, relying exclusively on God's name and the pittance of their senses, they go on living as wretchedly as usual. That excellent and most beautiful Spouse, however, seeks other men, or better, other souls not happy with just getting on, but satisfied only by a happy life, and therefore worthy of his marriage bed. Return to the Muses.
L. – But truly, do you know what I would have you do? Speak your mind.
A. – You were about to relate the point when Thisbe kills herself over Pyramus's half-dead body, who had fatally wounded himself

illius foedae libidinis et incendiorum venenatorum exsecrationem, quibus miseranda illa contingunt, deinde totus attollere in laude puri et sinceri amoris, quo animae dotatae disciplinis et virtute formosae copulantur intellectui per philosophiam et non solum mortem fugiunt, verum etiam vita beatissima perfruuntur.

Hinc ille tacitus ac diu consideratione nutans, motato capite abscessit.

25. Deinde ego quoque surrexi, redditisque pro Deo quotidianis votis, ire coeperamus in balneas (ille enim locus nobis, cum coelo tristi in agro esse minime poteramus, aptus ad disputandum et familiaris fuit) cum ecce ante fores advertimus gallos gallinaceos ineuntes pugnam nimis acrem. Libuit attendere. Quid enim non ambiunt, qua non peragrant oculi amantum, ne quid undeunde innuat pulchritudo rationis cuncta scientia et nescientia modificantis et gubernantis, quae inhiantes sibi sectatores suos trahit quacumque atque ubicumque se quaeri iubet? Nam unde aut ubi non potest signum dare? Ut in eisdem ipsis gallis erat videre intenta proiectius capita, inflatas comas, vehementes ictus, cautissimas evitationes, et in omni motu animalium rationis expertium nihil non decorum, quippe alia ratione desuper omnia moderante. Postremo legem ipsam victoris: superbum cantum et membra in unum quasi orbem collecta velut in fastum dominationis. Signum autem victi: elatas a cervice pennulas, et in voce atque motu deforme totum et eo ipso naturae legibus nescio quomodo concinnum et pulchrum.

26. Multa quaerebamus: cur sic omnes, cur propter dominationem in subiectas sibi feminas, cur deinde nos ipsa pugnae facies aliquantum et praeter altiorem istam considerationem duceret in voluptatem spectaculi: quid in nobis esset quod a sensibus remota multa quaereret: quid rursum quod ipsorum sensuum invitatione caperetur. Dicebamus nobis ipsis: Ubi non lex? Ubi non meliori debitum imperium? Ubi non umbra constantiae? Ubi non imitatio verissimae illius pulchritudinis? Ubi non modus? Atque inde admoniti ut spectandi modus esset, perreximus quo propositum erat. Atque ibi, ut potuimus, sane diligenter (nam et recentes res

in error. At that point, the emotional climax of the story, you have your opportunity. Consider the curse of that unclean lust and poisoned passion as the basis for that miserable end. Then turn to praising that clean and sincere love by which disciplined characters made beautiful by virtue are raised up by a philosophical mind. In so doing they not only escape death, but enjoy the happiest of lives.

Licentius became silent, reflected a while, nodded, and then retired.

25. I also got up, said my daily prayers, and all of us started moving to the baths. There we used to do a lot of talk, for it was comfortable, especially when the weather did not allow us to meet outdoors. All of a sudden we came across a cock fight, and eagerly watched. What wouldn't lovers of truth and beauty be eager to see and search out? Isn't any such occasion good enough to bring the beauty of reason to bear on things known and unknown, and let it attract its followers wherever and however it can? Cannot signs of it be seen anywhere and coming from anywhere? Take that cock fight. We could see their intent heads stretched forward, hackles raised, mighty thrusts of beak and spur, uncanny dodgings. There was nothing amiss in every motion of those irrational beasts. There was clearly another Reason controlling everything from on high, down to the universal law of victor and vanquished. The first crowed in triumph and puffed its feathers in a clear sign of superiority. The other had ended up with a featherless neck, voiceless, and crippled. I don't know how, but everything was a hymn to the beauty and harmony of nature.

26. We asked a lot of questions. Why should there always be fights over the possession of females? Why was the fight so attractive as to bring us down from our lofty thoughts to the pleasure of watching it? What inner impulse forces us to seek realities way beyond the senses? What, inside us, gets enticed by the senses themselves? We were musing: Where is there no law? Where does the victor not get power over the defeated? Where is there no blotch spoiling regularity? Where is there anything failing to imitate the beauty of things? Where is there no measure? Startled into realizing that there should also be measure in watching those fowl, we went

erant, et quando poterant tam insignita trium studiosorum memoriam effugere?) omnia nostrae lucubrationis opuscula in hanc libelli partem contulimus. Nihilque a me aliud actum est illo die, ut valetudini parcerem, nisi quod ante coenam cum ipsis dimidium volumen Virgilii audire quotidie solitus eram, nihil nobis ubique aliud quam rerum modum considerantibus. Quem non probare nemo potest; sentire autem, cum quisque aliquid studiose agit, difficillimum atque rarissimum.

DISPUTATIO SECUNDA

CAPUT IX
Ordo dux ad Deum

27. Deinde postridie bene mane alacres ad solitum locum convenimus in eoque consedimus. Et ego attentis in me ambobus:

A. – Hic esto, inquam, Licenti, quantum potes, et tu quidem, Trygeti; nec enim parva res agitur: de ordine quaerimus. Quid ego nunc quasi in schola illa, unde me quoquo modo evasisse gaudeo, constitutus copiose atque ornate vobis ordinem laudem? Accipite, si vultis, imo facite ut velitis, quo neque quidquam de huius laude brevius neque ut mihi videtur verius dici potest. Ordo est quem si tenuerimus in vita, perducet ad Deum, et quem nisi tenuerimus in vita, non perveniemus ad Deum. Perventuros autem nos iam, nisi me animus de vobis fallit, praesumimus et speramus. Diligentissime igitur inter nos ista questio versari debet atque dissolvi.

Vellem adessent caeteri qui nobiscum his negotiis solent interesse. Vellem, si fieri posset, non istos tantum, sed omnes saltem familiares nostros, quorum semper admiror ingenium, nunc mecum habere quam vos estis intentos; aut certe ipsum tantum Zenobium, quem de hac re tanta molientem numquam pro eius magnitudine otiosus accepi. Sed quia id non evenit, legent litteras nostras, quoniam instituimus iam de istis rebus verba non perdere resque ipsas a memoria fugaces, scriptorum quasi vinculo quo reducantur innectere. Et sic fortasse ordo ipse poscebat, qui eorum

where we had intended. As soon as possible, we compiled there this part of the book containing the matter discussed the previous night. The three of us could hardly forget the important things that had happened so recently. Because of my poor health, I didn't do anything more that day, except listening to about half a book by Virgil just before dinner, as was my daily habit. We spoke of nothing else but the mode of being of things. Everybody approves of it, but to do it is another matter, most difficult and rare indeed.

SECOND DEBATE

NINE
Order leads to God

27. Early next day we met in the usual place and sat down ready to work. The eyes of both were riveted on me.

A. – Pay attention as best you can, Licentius, and you too, Trygetius. We are going to talk about nothing less than order. Now should I really sing the praises of order to you in that cumbersome and ornate language of my former rhetoric school, which I was so eager to run away from? Believe it or not, nothing will be shorter or truer than what I am going to say. Order is what leads us to God, provided we keep it in life. Should we fail in keeping it, we shall not get to see God. Unless I be wrong about you, we can take for granted and hope that we shall get there. Let us therefore thrash out this matter and solve all its related problems.

I wish those who share with us this same interest were here. At least I would wish that all those friends of ours whose mind I admire were here with me, as attentive as you are now. Certainly I should have liked to see here Zenobius, for whom I never had the time when he was occupied with this great question. But as it didn't happen, he and the others will read our notes. Luckily we decided not to allow any word of this debate to be lost. We shall tie all things that tend to slip from memory with the string of writing, as it were, to make them retrievable. Even our friends' absence is part of order, perhaps. As such a great task has fallen

procuravit absentiam. Nam et vos profecto in rem tantam, quia solis perferenda imponitur nobis, erectiore animo insurgitis et cum illi legerint qui nobis maxima cura sunt, si quid eos moverit ad contradicendum, alias nobis disputationes disputatio ista procreabit seque ipsa successio sermonum in ordinem inseret disciplinae. Sed nunc, ut promiseram, Licentio quantum res patitur adversabor, qui totam causam iam pene confecit, si posset eam defensionis muro stabiliter firmeque vallare.

CAPUT X
Ordo quid. Ut coercendi aemulationis et inanis iactantiae motus in adolescentibus, qui dant operam litteris.

28. Hic ubi eos, silentio, vultu, oculis, suspensione atque immobilitate membrorum et rei magnitudine satis commotos et audiendi desiderio inflammatos esse conspexi:

A. – Ergo, inquam, Licenti, si tibi videtur, collige in te quidquid virium potes, elima quidquid habes acuminis et ordo iste quid sit definitione complectere.

Tum ille ubi se ad definiendum cogi audivit, quasi aqua frigida aspersus exhorruit et turbatione vultu me intuens atque, ut fit, ipsa trepidatione subridens:
L. – Quid hoc est rei? Quid quasi tibi videor?, inquit, adnuere? Nescio quo adventitio spiritu me credis inflatum? (Statimque sese animans): – Aut fortasse, ait, aliquid mecum est.

Paululumque siluit, ut in definitionem quidquid illi de ordine notionis erat, conduceretur. Deinde erectior:
L. – Ordo est, inquit, per quem aguntur omnia quae Deus constituit.

29. A. – Quid ipse Deus, inquam, non tibi videtur agi ordine?
L. – Prorsus, inquit, videtur.
T. – Ergo agitur Deus, ait Trygetius.
L. – Et ille: Quid enim, inquit, Christum Deum negas, qui et ordine ad nos venit, et a Patre Deo missum esse se dicit? Si igitur Deus Christum ordine ad nos misit et Deum Christum esse non negamus, non solum agit omnia, sed agitur ordine etiam Deus.

on our shoulders alone, you sharpen your attention all the more. As they read our carefully drafted notes, and are moved to fiercely criticizing something in them, this debate will beget more debates, and by putting them together they will form an ordered body of doctrine. But now, as I had promised, I will attack Licentius as hard as his thesis can bear. He has almost completed his case, so let us see if he can protect it with a strong defensive wall.

TEN

What order is. How to spur the sense of emulation and vainglory in teenagers who undertake the liberal arts.

28. I watched them in silence, their motionless faces and staring eyes betraying their burning wish to be instructed in a matter of such magnitude.

A. – Licentius, if you please, gather together all the strength you have, sharpen your wits and define order for me.

On hearing that he was being caught into having to craft a definition, first he cringed as if under a shower of cold water, then, half perturbed and half smiling, he turned to me.

L. – What is that? What do you take me for? Am I right in thinking you believe there is something the matter with me? (Then, suddenly taking heart): Perhaps there is something in me after all.

There followed a brief silence, during which he concentrated on his definition of order. Then he stood up and said:

L. – Order is the government of all things put in place by God.

29. A. – What about God himself. Don't you think he is subjected to order?

L. – I certainly think so.

T. – Therefore God is governed.

L. – As Christ himself said, he came to us in the order established by God the Father who sent Him. Would you deny that Christ is God on those grounds? If God then sent us Christ according to

T. – Hic Trygetius addubitans: – Nescio, inquit, quomodo istuc accipiam. Deum enim quando nominamus, non quasi mentibus ipse Christus occurrit, sed Pater. Ille autem tunc occurrit, quando Dei Filium nominamus.
L. – Bellam rem facis, inquit Licentius. Negabimus ergo Dei Filium Deum esse?

Hic ille, cum ei respondere periculosum videretur, tamen se coegit atque ait:
T. – Et hic quidem Deus est, sed tamen proprie Patrem Deum dicimus.
A. – Cui ego: – Cohibe te potius, inquam; non enim Filius improprie Deus dicitur.

At ille religione commotus, cum etiam verba sua scripta esse nollet, urgebat Licentius ut manerent, puerorum scilicet more vel potius hominum, proh nefas! pene omnium, quasi vero gloriandi causa inter nos illud ageretur. Cuius motum animi cum obiurgarem gravioribus verbis, erubuit: qua eius perturbatione animadvertit ridentem laetantemque Trygetium. Et ambobus:
A. – Itane agitis?, inquam. Nonne vos movet quibus vitiorum molibus atque imperitiae tenebris premamur et cooperiamur? Haeccine est illa paulo ante vestra, de qua ineptus laetabar, attentio et in Deum veritatemque surrectio? O si videretis, vel tam lippientibus oculis quam ego, in quibus periculis iaceamus, cuius morbi dementiam risus iste indicet! O si videretis, quam cito, quam statim quantoque productius eum verteretis in fletus. Miseri, nescitis ubi sumus? Demersos quidem esse animos omnium stultorum indoctorumque commune est, sed non uno atque eodem modo demersis opem sapientia et manum porrigit. Alii sunt, credite, alii sunt qui sursum vocantur, alii qui in profunda laxantur. Nolite, obsecro vos, geminare mihi miserias. Satis mihi sint vulnera mea, quae ut sanentur, pene quotidianis fletibus Deum rogans, indigniorem tamen esse me qui tam cito saner quam volo saepe memetipse convinco. Nolite, obsecro, si quid mihi amoris, si quid necessitudinis debetis, si intellegitis quantum vos diligam, quanti faciam, quantum me cura exagitet morum vestrorum, si dignus sum quem non negligatis, si denique, Deo teste, non mentior, nihil me plus mihi optare quam vobis, rependite mihi beneficium, et si me magistrum libenter vocatis, reddite mihi mercedem: boni estote.

order, and we don't deny that Christ is God, we must admit that God not only governs, but is also governed.

T. (perplexed) – I don't know how this can happen. When we say "God" we usually mean God the Father, not Christ. What you said applies to God the Son.

L. – That's a good one! Shall we deny then that God's Son is God?

Trygetius sensed the danger of a hasty reply, and kept quiet. Then:

T. – He is also God but, properly speaking, by "God" we mean the Father.

A. – Say no more; the Son is also properly called God.

Pious as he was, Trygetius didn't want his words recorded, but Licentius insisted that they be. It is not only boys who think that a debate is for winning glory. Grown-ups think the same; unfortunately almost all do. He blushed when I scolded him hard, as Trygetius smiled, delighted. I spoke to both:

A. – What are you doing? Aren't you troubled by the immense load of vice we bear and by the darkness of ignorance enveloping us? Where is your attentiveness and eagerness for God's truth that I was rash enough to praise such a short while ago? If you could only see, even through bleary eyes like mine, what dangers surround us, what mental sickness lurks behind that laughter! If you glimpsed it, how quickly, immediately, and for how long would you turn it into weeping. Poor friends, don't you know our situation? Prostration of soul is the common lot of all fools and the unlearned, but they don't get wisdom's resources and helping hand in one and the same way. Some are indeed rescued from those depths, but others are left to rot there. Please don't double my grief. My own wounds are enough. I pray God every day, at times even weeping, to have them healed, even though I judge myself unworthy of being healed as quickly as I wish. So please don't do it. If you love me, if you owe me any friendship, if you understand my love for you and how much I am ready to do for you, how much I care for your behavior and am worthy of not being neglected by you; and finally, if I swear by God that I don't wish for myself anything more than I wish for you, and if you willingly have me as a teacher, pay me this fee: behave.

30. Hic ubi, ne plura dicerem, lacrymae mihi modum imposuerunt, Licentius molestissime ferens quod omnia scribebantur:

L. – Quid enim, ait, fecimus, oro te?
A. – Adhuc, inquam, nec fateris saltem peccatum tuum? Tu nescis in illa schola graviter me stomachari solitum, quod usque adeo pueri non utilitate atque decore disciplinarum, sed inanissimae laudis amore ducerentur, ut quosdam etiam aliena verba recitare non puderet exciperentque plausus (o ingemiscendum malum!) ab eisdem ipsis quorum erant illa quae recitabant. Ita vos, quamvis nihil unquam, ut opinor, tale feceritis, tamen et in philosophiam, et in eam vitam quam me tandem occupasse laetor, aemulationis tabificae atque inanis iactantiae ultimam, sed nocentiorem caeteris omnibus pestem introducere ac proseminare conamini: et fortasse, quia vobis ab ista vanitate morboque deterreo, pigriores eritis ad studia doctrinae et ab ardore ventosae famae repercussi in torporem inertiae congelabitis. Me miserum, si necesse erit tales etiam nunc perpeti, a quibus vitia decedere sine aliorum vitiorum successione non possint.
L. – Probabis, ait Licentius, quam purgatiores futuri simus. Modo illud obsecramus, per omnia quae diligis, ut ignotum nobis velis atque illa omnia deleri iubeas, simul, ut parcas etiam tabulis, quas iam non habemus. Non enim aliquid in libros translatum est eorum quae a nobis multa disserta sunt.
T. – Prorsus, inquit Trygetius, maneat nostra poena, ut ea ipsa quae nos illicit fama, flagello proprio a suo amore deterreat. Ut enim solis amicis et familiaribus nostris litterae istae innotescant, non parum desudabimus.

Assensus est ille.

CAPUT XI
Monnica ob sexum non arcenda a philosophica disputatione

31. Atque interea mater ingressa est, quaesivitque a nobis quid promovissemus; nam et ei quaestio nota erat. Cuius et ingressum et rogationem cum scribi nostro more iussissem:

30. As my tears prevented me from saying anything more, Licentius felt most hurt that we were writing all that.

L. – What was wrong with that?
A. – Don't you see your fault yet? You have no idea how disgusted I was in that school. Boys were led to learn not by the usefulness and beauty of the subjects, but by the love of vain praise. It was dreadful to see them shamelessly recite other people's writings in order to get their applause! I don't think you yourselves have ever done such a thing. Nevertheless you are trying to introduce into philosophy, and into that lifestyle which I have at last adopted, the woodworm of emulation and empty boasting. It is the lowliest kind of plague, but more noxious and contagious than all the others. But were I to deter you from such morbid vanity, you would perhaps become slothful for sound doctrine. You would fall from the burning desire for vain reputation down to the frozen torpor of inaction. Poor me, having to bear characters who cannot get rid of one vice without falling into another.
L. – You'll see how much we shall improve. But now please, for love's sake, forgive us and order that all this mess be deleted from the records. It is a way of being merciful to the writing tablets also, for we have run out of them. As yet none of the many things we have debated has been transcribed into the books.
T. – Rather, let our punishment remain. Our having been enticed by vainglory will act as a deterrent for others. Even if only friends and relatives come to read it, it will be hard work just the same.
Licentius agreed.

ELEVEN
Monica is not excluded from the debate on the grounds of her sex

31. In the meantime my mother came in, asking how far we had gone. She knew what we had been discussing. At once I ordered her to come in and her question to be recorded as was our custom.

M. – Quid agitis, inquit? Numquidnam in illis quos legitis libris etiam feminas unquam audivi in hoc genus disputationis inductas? **A.** Cui ego:– Non valde curo, inquam, superborum imperitorumque iudicia, qui similiter in legendos libros atque in salutandos homines irruunt. Non enim cogitant quales ipsi, sed qualibus induti vestibus sint et quanta pompa rerum fortunaeque praefulgeant. Isti enim in litteris non multum attendunt aut unde sit quaestio aut quo pervenire disserentes moliantur, quidve ab eis explicatum atque confectum sit. In quibus tamen quia nonnulli reperiuntur animi contemnendi non sunt (aspersi sunt enim quibusdam condimentis humanitatis et facile per aureas depictasque ianuas ad sacrosancta philosophiae penetralia perducuntur) satis eis fecerunt et maiores nostri, quorum libros tibi nobis legentibus notos esse video.

Et his temporibus, ut omittam caeteros, vir et ingenio et eloquentia et ipsis insignibus muneribusque fortunae, et, quod ante omnia est, mente praestantissimus Theodorus, quem bene ipsa nosti, id agit, ut et nunc et apud posteros nullum genus hominum de litteris nostrorum temporum iure conqueratur. Mei autem libri si quorum forte manus tetigerint lectoque meo nomine non dixerint: "*Iste quis est?*", codicemque proiecerint, sed vel curiosi vel nimium studiosi contempta vilitate liminis intrare perrexerint, me tecum philosophantem non moleste ferent nec quemquam istorum quorum meis litteris sermo miscetur, fortasse contemnent. Sunt enim non solum liberi, quod cuivis disciplinae liberali, nedum philosophiae satis est, sed summo apud suos loco nati. Doctissimorum autem hominum litterae etiam sutores philosophatos et multo viliora fortunarum genera continent: qui tamen tanta ingenii virtutisque luce fulserunt, ut bona sua cum qualibet huiuscemodi nobilitate nullo modo vellent, etiamsi possent, ulla conditione mutare. Nec deerit, mihi crede, tale hominum genus cui plus placeat hoc ipsum, quia mecum philosopharis, quam si quid hic aliud aut iucunditatis aut gravitatis invenerit. Nam et feminae sunt apud veteres philosophatae, et philosophia tua mihi plurimum placet.

32. Nam ne quid, mater, ignores, hoc graecum verbum quo *philosophia* nominatur, latine *amor sapientiae* dicitur. Unde etiam

M. – What are you doing? I have never read of women entering into such debates in any of your books.
A. – I don't give two hoots about the judgment of the proud and the ignorant. They rush into reading books as into kowtowing to men. They pay no attention to human qualities, but to clothes, pomp, and the ephemeral circumstances of well being. When they read, they don't care much about what is being written about, or what the author is trying to get at, or what he explains or accomplishes. There are some to be found among these, however, who are not to be despised. They get a sprinkling of culture, somehow managing to enter through gilded and painted gates into the inner sanctum of philosophy. Our ancestors wrote for their sake, and I see that you are acquainted with their books through our reading them.

Of our own days I will only mention Theodore, a man you know well. He is endowed with a good mind, eloquence and economic means, and an excellent character. He is so good, that neither today nor in the future will anyone complain of the literature of our own days. As to my books, it is possible that they fall into somebody's hands who, on reading my name, may ask "Who's that?" and fling the book away. If not, curiosity or studiousness will entice them through a rather modest gate. On entering, they will not be troubled to find me talking philosophy with you, nor would they despise the characters whose talk appears in my writings. They are not only free, a necessary condition for philosophy as for any of the other liberal arts, but people of high station. The writings of many learned men contain stories of shoemakers given to philosophy, and of men of even lowlier station. They shone with such a light of mind and virtue that, even given the chance of bartering their social status with that of the nobility they wouldn't take it. And there will be some, believe me, who will find my talking with you here more pleasing than finding platitudes or high-brow stuff. There were plenty of philosopher-women in ancient times, and I rather like *your* philosophy.

32. For you to know, mother, "philosophy" is a word of Greek origin meaning "love of wisdom." That is why even divinely

divinae Scripturae, quas vehementer amplecteris, non omnino philosophos, sed philosophos huius mundi evitandos atque irridendos esse praecipiunt. Esse autem alium mundum ab istis oculis remotissimum, quem paucorum sanorum intellectus intuetur, satis ipse Christus significat, qui non dicit: *Regnum meum non est de mundo*, sed: *Regnum meum non est de hoc mundo*. Nam quisquis omnem philosophiam fugiendam putat, nihil nos vult aliud quam non amare sapientiam. Contemnerem te igitur in his litteris meis, si sapientiam non amares; non autem contemnerem, si eam mediocriter amares, multo minus, si tantum quantum ego amares sapientiam. Nunc vero cum eam multo plus quam meipsum diligas, et noverim quantum me diligas, cumque in ea tantum profeceris, ut iam nec cuiusvis incommodi fortuiti nec ipsius mortis, quod viris doctissimis difficillimum est, horrore terrearis, quam summam philosophiae arcem omnes esse confitentur, egone me non libenter tibi etiam discipulum dabo?

33. Hic illa cum blande ac religiose numquam me tantum mentitum esse dixisset et viderem tam multa nos verba fudisse, ut neque scribenda non essent et iam libri modus esset neque tabulae reliquae forent, placuit quaestionem differri, simul ut meo stomacho parcerem. Nam eum plus quam vellem commoverant et quae mihi emovenda in illos adolescentes necessario visa sunt. Sed cum abire coepissemus:

L. – Memento, inquit Licentius, quam multa et quam necessaria nobis abs te accipienda per occultissimum illum divinumque ordinem etiam te nesciente subministrentur.
A. – Video, inquam, et ingratus Deo non sum, vosque ipsos qui haec advertitis ob id ipsum praesumo fore meliores.

Hoc fuit tantum illo die negotium meum.

inspired scriptures, which you love so much, do not enjoin to avoid and make fun of all philosophers without distinction, but of the philosophers *of this world*. Christ himself makes the distinction between this world and another far removed from it, when saying: My kingdom is not of *this* world. He does not say: My kingdom is not of *the* world. Whoever condemns philosophy as a whole, condemns nothing less than wisdom itself. If you were not a lover of wisdom, I would despise you in my writings. I would not despise you, however, were you to love it even half-heartedly. Much less would I do such a thing if you loved wisdom as much as I do. As a matter of fact you love it far more than you love me, and do I know how much you love me! You love it so much, indeed, that neither setbacks of any kind nor death itself holds any terror for you. The learned are of the opinion that to achieve this most difficult state is the inner core of philosophy itself. Should I not therefore be your willing disciple?

33. At this point she said, with all the mother's gentleness she could muster, that I had never lied so much in my life. I, on my part, noticed that too many words needed to be put in writing, and that the length had already exceeded that of an average book, and we had run out of writing matter. We decided therefore to postpone the debate, and in passing to have mercy on my stomach. While going out, Licentius said:

L. – Remember how many and necessary things that most hidden and divine order has provided for us through you, even without your noticing it.
A. – I see, and I give thanks to God for making you notice such things. On these grounds I expect you to improve.

And we adjourned.

LIBER SECUNDUS

DISPUTATIO PRIMA

CAPUT I
Ordinis definitio expenditur

1. Interpositis deinde pauculis diebus venit Alypius, et exorto sole clarissimo invitavit caeli nitor et quantum in illis locis hieme poterat blanda temperies in pratum descendere, quo saepius et familiarius utebamur. Nobiscum erat etiam mater nostra, cuius ingenium atque res divinas inflammatum animum, cum antea convictu diuturno et diligenti considerationem perspexeram; tum vero in quadam disputatione non parvae rei, quam die natali meo cum conviviis habui atque in libellum contuli, tanta mihi mens eius apparuerat, ut nihil aptius verae philosophiae videretur. Itaque institueram, cum abundaret otio, agere ut colloquio nostro non deesset. Quod in primo etiam huius operis libro abs te cognitum est.

2. Cum igitur memorato in loco, ut commode potuimus, consedissemus, ego illi duobus adolescentibus:

A. – Quamvis vobis, inquam, succensuerim pueriliter de magnis rebus agentibus, tamen mihi videtur non sine ordine, propitio Deo, accidisse, quod in sermone quo vos ab ista levitate detrahebam, tempus ita consumptum est, ut res tanta ad Alypii adventum dilata videatur. Quapropter, quoniam ei iam quaestionem notissimam feci et quantum in ea processerimus ostendi, paratusne es, Licenti, causam quam suscepisti ex illa tua definitione defendere? Nam meminisse me arbitror te ordinem esse dixisse per quem Deus ageret omnia.
L. – Paratus sum, inquit, quantum valeo.
A. – Quomodo ergo, inquam, agit ordine omnia Deus? Itane ut etiam se ordine agat, an praeter eum ordine ab eo cetera gubernantur?
L. – Ubi omnia bona sunt, inquit, ordo non est. Est enim summa aequalitas, quae ordinem nihil desiderat.
A. – Negas, inquam, apud Deum omnia bona esse?

BOOK TWO

FIRST DEBATE

ONE
Analysis of the definition of order

1. A few days later Alypius arrived. After a splendid dawn the sky was so clear and the weather so mild for the season that we decided to sit down on the lawn, where we often freely met. My mother was with us. Living with her for so long, I had had occasion to observe her keen mind and burning love for things divine. On the celebration of my birthday with some friends we held a debate on some important matter, later put down in writing. There I verified the greatness of her mind, so that no other person seemed to me fitter for true philosophy. And so I coaxed her into being with us whenever she was not too busy. That is why she has already appeared in the first book of this work.

2. As we sat down and made ourselves comfortable as best we could in our usual place, I addressed the two youths:

A. – I was hard on you for dealing with matters of such importance in such a puerile fashion. This, however, did not happen without order. With God's help, the time spent in distracting you from such levity made it possible to delay the issue until the coming of Alypius. I have briefed him about the matter and our progress in it. Are you ready, Licentius, to defend the thesis stemming from your definition? I recall that you affirmed order to be the government of all things by God.
L. – I am ready or, better, "at" the ready.
A. – How does God do everything in order? Does He include Himself in that order, or is everything else governed by that order and He is not?
L. – Where everything is good there is no order. There is a maximum of equality, so order is irrelevant.
A. – Do you then deny that all good things are in God?

L. – Non nego, inquit.
A. – Conficitur, inquam, neque Deum neque illa quae apud Deum sunt, ordine administrari.

Concedebat.

A. – Numquidnam, inquam, omnia bona nihil tibi videntur esse?
L. – Imo, ait, ipsa vere sunt.
A. – Ubi est ergo, inquam, illud tuum quod dixisti, omnia quae sunt ordine administrari nihilque omnino esse quod ab ordine separatum sit?
L. – Sed sunt, inquit, etiam mala, per quae factum est ut bona ordo concludat; nam sola bona non ordinem reguntur, sed simul bona et mala. Quum autem dicimus: Omnia quae sunt, non sola utique bona dicimus. Ex quo fit ut omnia simul, quae Deus administrat, ordine administrentur.

Cui ego:

3. A. Quae administrantur et aguntur, videntur tibi moveri an immobilia putas esse?
L. – Ista, inquit, quae in hoc fiunt mundo, fateor moveri.
A. – Reliqua, inquam, negas?
L. – Quae sunt cum Deo, inquit, non moventur; reliqua omnia moveri arbitror.
A. – Cum igitur ea quae cum Deo sunt, inquam, non moveri putas, caetera autem concedis moveri, ostendis omnia quae moventur non esse cum Deo.
L. – Repete hoc ipsum, inquit, paulo planius.

Quod non mihi visus est difficultate intellegendi fieri voluisse, sed quaerenti spatium quo inveniret quid responderet.

A. – Dixisti, inquam, ea quae cum Deo sunt non moveri, caetera autem moveri. Si ergo quae moventur non moverentur si essent cum Deo, quoniam omnia quae sunt cum Deo negas moveri, restat ut praeter Deum sint quae moventur.

Quibus dictis adhuc tacebat, cum tandem:

L. – Videtur mihi, inquit, quod et in hoc mundo si qua non moventur, cum Deo sunt.
A. – Nihil hoc ad me, inquam. Fateris enim, ut opinor, non omnia quae in hoc mundo sunt non moveri. Ex quo conficitur non omnia mundi huius esse cum Deo.

L. – I don't.
A. – It follows then that neither God nor divine things are directed within an order.

He agreed.

A. – Are all good things nothing, then, according to you?
L. – On the contrary, they truly exist.
A. – How come, then, that you affirmed everything to be included in order without exception?
L. – But there are also evil things. It is because of them that order must include the good ones. The latter by themselves would not need order. They need it together with the evil ones. On talking of all things that are, we don't mean the good ones exclusively. God administers both good and evil.

3. **A.** – Are things arrayed to happen in an unstable or in a stable manner? What do you think?
L. – The things of this world are unstable, I must admit.
A. – Do you deny that for the rest?
L. – Things with God are stable. All else, I think, is unstable.
A. – Therefore if things with God are stable according to you, and the rest are not, you show that all unstable things are not with God.
L. – Say it again, a little more clearly.

I saw that he had understood, but was bargaining for time to think what to say.

A. – You stated that things with God are stable; the rest are not. Therefore if the unstable ones were to become stable by being with God (you deny that things with God change), instability would be altogether outside God.

He kept silent for a while. Then:

L. – I would say that even things of this world can be with God if they be stable.
A. – Don't tell me stories. You stated, I think, that not everything in this world is stable. From this it follows that not everything in this world is with God.
L. – Yes, not everything.

L. – Fateor, inquit, non omnia.
A. – Ergo est aliquid sine Deo.
L. – Non, inquit.
A. – Cum Deo sunt igitur omnia.
L. – Hic cunctabundus: Quaeso, inquit, illud non dixerim, quod sine Deo nihil sit; nam prorsus omnia quae moventur, non mihi videntur esse cum Deo.
A. – Sine Deo est, inquam, igitur coelum hoc, quod moveri nemo ambigit.
L. – Non est, inquit, sine Deo coelum.
A. – Ergo est aliquid cum Deo, quod moveatur.
L. – Non possum, inquit, ut volo, explicare quod sentio: tamen quid moliar dicere, peto ut non exspectatis verbis meis sagacissime, si potestis, intellegatis. Nam et sine Deo mihi nihil videtur esse, et quod cum Deo est, rursum videtur inconcussum manere: coelum autem dicere sine Deo esse non possum, non solum quod nihil sine Deo esse arbitror, sed quod coelum putem habere aliquid quod non movetur, quod vere aut Deus est aut cum Deo, quae iam sapiens intellegit quamvis ipsum coelum non dubitem verti ac moveri.

CAPUT II

Cum Deo esse, quid sit. Quomodo sapiens cum Deo manet immotus.

4. A. – Defini ergo, inquam, si placet, quid sit esse cum Deo et quid sit non esse sine Deo. Si enim de verbis inter nos controversia est, facile contemnetur, dummodo rem ipsam quam concepisti mente videamus.
L. – Odi ergo, inquit, definire.
A. – Quid ergo faciemus?, inquam.
L. – Tu, inquit, defini, quaeso. Nam facilius est mihi videre in alterius definitione quid non probem, quam quidquam bene definiendo explicare.
A. – Geram tibi morem, inquam. Videtur tibi id esse cum Deo quod ab eo regitur atque administratur?
L. – Non, ait ille, hoc animo conceperam, cum dicebam ea quae non moventur esse cum Deo.

A. – Therefore some things exist without God.
L. – No.
A. – But then everything must be with God.
L. (hesitatingly) – Please, I shouldn't have said that, for without God nothing is. But true enough, all unstable things seem to me not to be with God.
A. – The sky, then, exists without God, for no one contends that it is unstable.
L. – The sky does not exist without God.
A. – Therefore something exists with God to be changed by Him.
L. – I can't explain my thoughts as I want: nevertheless I would ask you not to be pedantic in understanding whatever I manage to say. What I think is that nothing exists without God, and again that what is with God remains firm. About the sky I cannot affirm that it exists without God, for I think nothing exists without Him. But I have a feeling that the sky has some stable foundation, whether it be God himself or something with Him, even though I do not doubt that it changes by moving cyclically.

TWO
What "to be with God" means. The wise man's stability in God.

4. **A.** – Would you please define, then, "to be with God" and "not to be without God"? It will be easy to spot whether we are arguing about words, provided we are shown what is in your mind.
L. – I hate defining.
A. – What shall we do, then?
L. – You define, please. It is much easier for me to spot something I do not agree with in someone else's definition, than to have to explain something defined by myself.
A. – As you wish. Are things directed and administered by God "with God"?
L. – No. This is what I meant when I said that stable things are with God.

A. – Vide ergo, inquam, utrum haec tibi saltem definitio placeat: cum Deo est quidquid intellegit Deum.
L. – Concedo, inquit.
A. – Quid ergo?, inquam. Sapiens tibi Deum intellegere non videtur?
L. – Videtur, inquit.
A. – Cum ergo sapientes non solum in una domo aut urbe, sed etiam per immensa regionum peregrinando navigandoque moveantur, quomodo erit verum quidquid cum Deo est non moveri?
L. – Risum mihi, inquit, movisti, quasi ego quod sapiens facit dixerim esse cum Deo. Cum Deo est, sed illud quod novit.
A. – Non novit, inquam, sapiens codicem suum, pallium, tunicam, supellectilem, si quam habet, caeteraque id genus, quae stulti etiam bene noverunt?
L. – Fateor, inquit, nosse tunicam et nosse pallium non esse cum Deo.

5. **A.** – Hoc ergo, inquam, dicis: Non omne quod novit sapiens esse cum Deo, sed tamen quidquid sapientis cum Deo est id nosse sapientem.
L. – Optime, inquit; nam quidquid sensu isto corporis novit non est cum Deo, sed illud quod animo percipit. Plus etiam fortasse audeo dicere; sed tamen dicam: vobis enim existimatoribus aut confirmer aut discam. Quisquis ea sola novit quae corporis sensus attingit, non solum cum Deo esse non mihi videtur, sed ne secum quidem.

Hic cum Trygetium animadvertissem in eo vultu, ut nescio quid velle dicere videretur, sed verecundia eum, ne quasi in alienum locum irrueret, contineri, feci potestatem, iam tacente Licentio, ut promeret si quid vellet. At ille:
T. – Ista, inquit, quae ad sensus corporis pertinent prorsus nemo mihi videtur nosse. Aliud est enim sentire, aliud nosse. Quare si quid novimus, solo intellectu contineri puto et eo solo posse comprehendi. Ex quo fit, ut si illud est cum Deo quod intellegendo sapiens novit, totum quod novit sapiens possit esse cum Deo.

Quod cum Licentius approbasset, subiecit aliud quod nullo pacto possem contemnere. Ait enim:

A. – See then, if you like, at least this definition: Whatever understands God is with God.
L. – Granted.
A. – Well, now. Don't you think a wise man understands God?
L. – I do.
A. – But even wise people are unstable. They move all the time at home, within a city, and wander on foot or by ship through immense regions of space. How can it be true that what is with God is stable?
L. (laughing)- Ha ha, as if I had dubbed the wise man's earthly activities "being with God." He is indeed with God insofar as he knows.
A. – But doesn't the wise man know his books, his clothes, whatever furniture he may possess, and such trinkets as fools also well know?
L. – All right, then. To know clothes like tunics and mantles is not "to be with God."

5. **A.** – What you are saying is, that not everything the wise man knows is "with God," but the wise man knows whatever of his is with God.
L. – Excellent. Not what he knows by means of his bodily senses is with God, but what he grasps with his soul. Perhaps what I am going to say is rash, but I will say it nevertheless. You judge, confirming or correcting. He who knows exclusively by means of bodily senses, not only seems to me not to be with God, but not even with himself.

Here I noticed that Trygetius wanted to say something, but was too shy to get into a fray that was not his own. I gave him leave to speak instead of Licentius, who was now silent.
T. – I don't think anyone "knows" things perceived by the senses. It is one thing to sense, another to know. For if we know something, I think it is by means of the intellect alone, where alone it can be understood. Therefore, if what the wise man knows by intellectual effort is "to be with God," everything he knows can be with God.

Licentius agreed, but submitted something else, which I could not ignore.

L. – Sapiens prorsus cum Deo est, nam et seipsum intellegit sapiens. Quod conficitur et ex eo quod a te accepi, id esse cum Deo, quod intellegit Deum, et ex eo quod a nobis dictum est, id esse cum Deo, quod a sapiente intellegitur. Sed hanc eius partem per quam istis utitur sensibus (non enim puto connumeranda esse, cum sapientem vocamus), fateor me nescire nec omnino cuiusmodi sit suspicari.

6. **A.** – Negas ergo, inquam, non solum ex corpore et anima, sed etiam ex anima tota constare sapientem, siquidem partem istam qua utitur sensibus, animae esse negare dementis est. Non enim ipsi oculi vel aures, sed nescio quid aliud per oculos sentit. Ipsum autem sentire si non damus intellectui, non damus alicui parti animae. Restat ut corpori tribuatur, quo absurdius dici nihil interim mihi videtur.

L. – Anima, inquit, sapientis perpurgata virtutibus et iam cohaerens Deo, sapientis etiam nomine digna est nec quidquam eius aliud delectat appellare sapientem: sed tamen quasi quaedam, ut ita dicam, sordes atque exuviae quibus se ille mundavit et quasi subtraxit in seipsum, ei animae serviunt; vel si tota haec anima dicenda est, ei certe parti animae serviunt atque subiectae sunt, quam solam sapientem nominari decet. In qua parte subiecta etiam ipsam memoriam puto habitare. Utitur ergo hac sapiens quasi servo, ut haec ei iubeat easque iam domito atque substrato metas legis imponat, ut dum istis sensibus utitur propter illa quae iam non sapienti, sed sibi sunt necessaria, non se audeat extollere nec superbire domino nec ipsis quae ad se pertinent passim atque immoderate uti. Ad illam enim vilissimam partem possunt ea pertinere quae praetereunt. Quibus autem est memoria necessaria, nisi praetereuntibus et quasi fugientibus rebus? Ille igitur sapiens amplectitur Deum eoque perfruitur qui semper manet, nec expectatur ut sit nec metuitur ne desit, sed eo ipso quo vere est, semper est praesens. Curat autem immobilis et in se manens servi sui quodammodo peculium, ut eo tamquam frugi et diligens famulus bene utatur parceque custodiat.

7. Quam sententiam eius cum admiratione considerans, recordatus sum idipsum aliquando me breviter illo audiente dixisse. Tum arridens:

L. – The wise man is certainly with God insofar as he understands himself. This follows from what I have heard you say, that to be with God is to understand God, plus what we have also affirmed, that whatever the wise man knows is also with God. But whichever part of the wise man makes use of the senses (not really relevant) I must confess not to know, nor even to suspect what it might be.

6. A. – Therefore you deny that the wise man consists of soul and body. You also deny to the soul the status of a whole. It would be the height of folly to deny that the senses escape the soul's control. It is not the eyes or the ears that sense, but something else that senses through them. And if it is not the mind, it cannot be the soul either. We must assign such powers to the body; this is the most absurd proposition I ever heard.
L. – The soul of the wise man, thoroughly cleansed by virtue and already clinging to God, can be truly called "wise." Nothing else in him can. Although it is the higher part of the soul that can truly be called wise, it still houses in its lower part the remains of what I may call the rubbish and dirt it sloughed off by withdrawing into itself. These are subjected to the soul and serve it. I am of the opinion that memory is one of these subservient parts. The wise man uses it as a slave, first by giving commands, and afterwards by imposing limits once the slave is sufficiently trained. This is to prevent memory from acting not for the benefit of the wise person, but for its own, thus placing itself above its station, acting against its master and using its own powers in a helter-skelter fashion or immoderately. Fleeting realities also belong to this lower part. What is memory for, if not for such impermanent realities? The truly wise clings to God and enjoys His permanent presence without hankering after it or fearing its possible disappearance. For God, being absolutely true, is also permanently present. Forever unmoved and immanent, He takes care in a certain measure of His servant's allowance, to be used well and frugally by him.

7. Impressed by what he had just said, I remembered having briefly said the same thing in his presence some time ago. I said:

A. – Gratias age, inquam, Licenti, huic servo tuo, qui tibi nisi aliquid de peculio suo ministraret, nunc fortasse quod promeres non haberes. Nam si ad eam partem memoria pertinet, quae se velut famulam bonae menti regendam concedit, ipsa nunc adiutus es, mihi crede, ut hoc diceres. Ergo antequam ad illum ordinem redeam, nonne tibi videtur vel propter talia, id est propter honestas ac necessarias disciplinas, memoria opus esse sapienti?
L. – Quid, inquit, memoria opus est, cum omnes suas res praesentes habeat ac teneat? Non enim vel in ipso sensu, ad id quod ante oculos nostros est, in auxilium vocamus memoriam. Sapienti ergo ante illos interiores intellectus oculos habenti omnia, id est Deum ipsum fixe immobiliterque intuenti, cum quo sunt omnia quae intellectus videt ac possidet, quid opus est, quaeso, memoria? Mihi autem ut opus esset ad haec quae abs te audieram retinenda, nondum sum illius famuli dominus, sed ei modo servio, modo pugno ut non serviam et quasi me audeo asserere in libertatem meam. Et si forte aliquando impero atque obtemperat mihi facitque saepe putare quod vicerim, in aliis rursus rebus ita sese erigit, ut eius sub pedibus miser iaceam. Quamobrem, quando de sapiente quaerimus, me nolo nomines.
A. – Nec me, inquam. Sed tamen numquidnam sapiens iste suos potest deserere, aut ullo pacto, cum hoc corpus agit, in quo istum famulum sua lege devinctum tenet, relinquet officium beneficia tribuendi quibus potest et maxime, quod ab eo vehementissime flagitatur, sapientiam ipsam docendi? Quod cum facit, ut congrue doceat minusque ineptus sit, praeparat saepe aliquid, quod ex dispositione eloquatur ac disputet, quod nisi memoriae commendaverit, pereat necesse est.

Ergo aut officia benevolentiae negabis esse sapientis, aut confiteberis res aliquas sapientis memoria custodiri. An fortasse aliquid suarum rerum non propter se quidem, sed propter suos sibi tamen necessarium commendat servandum illi famulo, ut ille tamquam sobrius et ex optima domini disciplina, non quidem custodiat, nisi quod propter stultos ad sapientiam perducendos, sed quod ei tamen ille custodiendum imperarit?
L. – Nec omnino huic, inquit, commendari quidquam arbitror a sapiente, siquidem ille semper Deo infixus est, sive tacitus, sive cum hominibus loquens: sed ille servus iam bene institutus diligenter

A. – Licentius, give thanks to this slave of yours. Had it not advanced you any of its allowance, you would have nothing to show for it. If memory truly acts as a slave of a good mind, it has just helped you to say what you did, believe me. So before we go back to the issue of order, don't you think that the wise man needs memory precisely as an aid to worthy and necessary disciplines?
L. – Why should he need memory? He has everything before the eyes of the mind. In fact in the realm of sentient knowledge, with things before our eyes, we do not make use of memory. Now a wise man has everything before the eyes of the mind. "Everything" means God himself grasped in a fixed and immutable glance, plus all the reality seen in God and grasped by the mind itself. What is memory for, in this case? In my case it should help me to retain all I hear from you, but I am not yet the master of that slave. At times in fact it is I who serve it, at other times I struggle not to serve it in an attempt to assert my freedom. At times I win, it obeys me, and gives me the illusion of having conquered. At other times, and in different matters, it stands over me, forcing me to grovel at its feet. Therefore, don't count me among the wise.
A. – Don't count me either. Nevertheless the wise man may not abandon his own. He controls the body, within which he holds this slave in chains by the body's own law. Even so, can he really neglect the duty to help whom he can, and above all what is most forcibly required of him: to teach wisdom? Now to teach properly and to improve in it, he must often prepare classes for delivery and discussion. Unless he committed all to memory, he would surely be lost. Therefore either you deny that the wise man ought to do good to others, or you admit that he must commit some matter to memory. After all, it is not for his own sake that he entrusts to memory what he needs, but for the sake of his own. And would memory, prudent in its turn under the master's strict discipline, keep that matter for itself, or rather use it for leading fools to wisdom, which is the task the master ordered in the first place?
L. – I don't think the wise man entrusts even that to memory. Whether silent or speaking to people, he is constantly immersed in God. The slave, memory, when well trained, hands him whatever

servat quod interdum disputanti domino suggerat et ei tamquam iustissimo gratum faciat officium suum, sub cuius se videt potestate vivere. Et hoc facit non quasi ratiocinando, sed summa illa lege summoque ordine praescribente.
A. – Nihil, inquam, nunc resisto rationibus tuis, quod suscepimus potius peragatur. De isto vero diligenter quemadmodum sese habeat (non enim parva res est aut tam parvo sermone contenta) videbimus alias, cum Deus ipse opportunitatem ordine dederit.

CAPUT III
Stultitia an cum Deo sit

8. **A.** Definitum est autem quid sit esse cum Deo. Et cum a me dictum esset, id esse cum Deo quod intellegit Deum, vos etiam plus adiecistis, ut ibi sint etiam illa quae intelleguntur a sapiente. Qua in re multum me movet quomodo subito cum Deo stultitia collocaveritis. Nam si cum Deo sunt quaecumque intellegit sapiens, nec nisi intellectam stultitiam effugere potest, erit etiam, quod dictu nefas est, pestis illa cum Deo.

Qua conclusione commoti, cum in silentio se aliquantum tenuissent:
T. – Respondeat, inquit Trygetius, etiam ille de cuius adventu ad istam disputationem opportunissimo non nos puto temere gratulatos.

Tum Alypius:
Al. – Deus meliora!, inquit. Huccine mihi tandem tantum meum silentium parabatur? Sed irrupta iam quies est. Verum nunc enitar huic utcumque rogationi satisfacere, cum mihi prius vel in futurum prospexero et a vobis impetravero ut a me amplius ista responsione nihil flagitetis.
A. – Nullo modo, inquam, est, Alypi, benevolentiae atque humanitatis tuae vocem tuam sermoni nostro etiam desideratam negare. Sed perge modo, quod instituisti effice; caetera, ut iam sese habet ordo ille, provenient.
Al. – Aeque mihi de ordine, inquit, sunt speranda meliora, in cuius assertione interim me substituere voluistis. Sed, ni fallor, ob hoc stultitiam Deo ista tua conclusione ab his copulatam putasti, quod

he needs for his discussion. It acts as a servant trying to please a most just master under whose authority it labors. This it does not by reasoning it out, but by a supreme law ordering and directing it.

A. – I won't answer your argument now. Let us carry our program through. It is weighty stuff, and not for such a short session. Let us postpone it, when God himself gives us the opportunity to analyze its details diligently and within a prescribed order.

THREE
Can foolishness be with God?

8. **A.** – We have then defined what "to be with God" means. To my asserting that whatever understands God is with God, you have added things understood by the wise. I am uneasy how quickly you have managed to link foolishness to God. For if whatever the wise man understands is with God, foolishness cannot escape being one of such things understood; whence it follows that even this plague, shocking to say, is also with God.

Stunned by this conclusion, they paused for a while. Then:

T. – It was timely to have invited Alypius here. Let him answer that.

Al. – God bless! Weren't you happy with my silence up until now? You have broken my peace. I will endeavor to answer, but not before warning you not to bother me with such questions in the future.

A. – Alypius, you are denying us our wish to have your voice join in the fray of the debate. This doesn't match either your good will or your usual good manners. But go on now, finish saying what you promised. The rest will find their appointed place in the order of things.

Al. – I am expecting better things from this order in whose interim defense you have driven me. If I am not mistaken, your conclusion linking foolishness to God stems from these two having affirmed that whatever the wise man understands is with God. Let us leave now how far this proposition might be accepted, and pay attention to your own reasoning. You said, "For if whatever the

universa quae intellegit sapiens cum Deo esse dixerunt. Sed id quatenus accipiendum sit nunc omitto; tuam illam ratiocinationem paululum adverte. Dixisti quippe: `*Nam si cum Deo sunt quaecumque intellegit sapiens, nec nisi intellectam stultitiam effugere potest.*' Quasi vero illud obscurum sit, antequam stultitiam quisque vitet, sapientis eum nomine non esse censendum. Et dictum est a sapiente intellecta esse cum Deo. Cum igitur evitandae stultitiae gratia eamdem stultitiam quisque intellegit, nondum est sapiens. Cum autem sapiens fuerit, non inter ea quae ille intellegit stultitia numeranda est. Quamobrem quoniam ea coniuncta sunt Deo, quae iam sapiens intellegit, recte a Deo stultitia secernitur.

9. A. – Acute quidem, inquam, ut soles, Alypi, respondisti, sed tamquam in alienas trusus angustias. Tamen quia, ut arbitror, adhuc mecum stultus esse dignaris, quid faciemus si quid aliquem nanciscamur sapientem, qui nos tanto malo docendo ac disputando libenter liberet? Nam nihil eum prius, quantum arbitror, deprecaturus sum, nisi ut mihi ostendas quae sit, quid sit, qualis sit omnino stultitia. De te enim non facile affirmaverim; me tamen tantum et tam diu detinet, quantum et quamdiu a me non intellegitur. Dicturus est ergo ille, te auctore: `*Ut hoc vos docerem, quando stultus eram ad me venire debuistis; modo autem vos vestri magistri esse poteritis, nam ego iam stultitiam non intellego.*' Quod quidem ab eo si audirem, non vererer admonere hominem ut comes nobis fieret simulque magistrum alium quaereremus. Ut enim plene stultitiam non intellego, video tamen nihil responsione hac esse stultius. Sed pudebit eum fortasse ita nos relinquere aut sequi. Disputabit ergo et exaggerabit copiosissime stultitiae mala. Nos autem bene nobis providentes, aut audiemus attente hominem nescientem quae loquatur, aut credemus eum id quod non intellegit scire, aut adhuc Deo susceptorum tuorum ratione stultitia copulata est. Nihil autem superiorum est quod video posse defendi. Restat igitur quod non vultis, extremum.

Al. – Numquam te, inquit, invidum senseram. Nam si ab istis, ut dicis, susceptis quidnam honorarii, ut solet, accepissem, dum ratiocinationis huius nimium tenax es, id eis modo reddere cogerer. Quare vel hoc contenti sint, quod me tecum laborante non parum eis ad excogitandum temporis dedi, vel, si victi patroni nulla quidem

wise understands is with God, foolishness cannot escape being one of such things understood." As if it was not clear that no one should be dubbed wise before avoiding foolishness. It has also been said that things understood by the wise are with God. Therefore, unless one avoids the very foolishness that one understands, one cannot be wise. The moment one becomes wise, one no longer has to understand foolishness. And since all things that the wise man understands are with God, foolishness can rightly be separated from God.

9. A. – Clever answer, Alypius, as usual, but you seem to have missed the point. If you agreed to become a fool like me, what should we do if a wise man willingly freed us from such a great evil with his teaching and debating? The first thing I would ask of him, I think, is to define foolishness, showing me what it really is. I don't know about you, but foolishness prevents *me* from progressing so much and for so long, to the extent by which I fail to understand it. In your view he would say: "To teach you that, you should have come to me when I was a fool myself; now you can teach yourselves, for I no longer understand what foolishness is." On hearing such an answer, I would ask him to become a co-learner with us, at once looking for another teacher for the three of us. I admit that I do not fully understand foolishness myself, but nothing would seem to me more foolish than such an answer. Perhaps he would be ashamed of leaving, or of following us. Launching into a harangue, he would exaggerate the evil of foolishness. Alert and on guard, we would either pay great attention to one who does not know what he is talking about, or would believe he knew things he did not understand, or would take it that foolishness is after all with God as you and your friends suppose. I don't see the plausibility of the first two. There remains the last, which you reject.
Al. – I would have never expected you to be so contentious. If I had got the usual fee from my friends, I would refund it now for your being unbeatable. But if they were happy at my performance with you, having given them time to think, or if they willingly

sua culpa consilio libenter auscultant, et in hoc iam tibi cedant et sint in caeteris cautiores.

10. A. – Non contemnam, inquam, quod in tua defensione Trygetius nescio quid etiam perstrepens dicere cupiebat, faciamque bona tua venia (nam fortasse bene instructus es, qui recens huic negotio supervenisti) ut remoto patrocinio ipsos causam suam peragentes audiam patienter, ut coeperam.

Tum Trygetius, Licentio prorsus absente:

T. – Quomodo vultis, inquit, accipite et ridete stultitiam meam. Non mihi videtur debere dici intellectus, quo intellegitur ipsa stultitia, quae non intellegendi vel sola vel maxima causa est.

A. – Non facile, inquam, recuso, istud accipere. Quamvis enim me multum moveat, quod sentit Alypius, quomodo recte possit quisque docere qualis sit res quam non intellegit quantamque menti afferat perniciem quod mente non videt (nam id utique attendens, quod tu dixisti dicere est veritus, cum ei sit ista etiam de doctorum libris nota sententia), tamen sensum ipsum considerans corporis, (nam et isto ipso anima utitur et ipsa sola est cum intellectu qualiscumque collatio) adducor ut dicam neminem posse videre tenebras. Quamobrem, si menti hoc est intellegere, quod sensui videre, et licet quisque oculis apertis, sanis purisque sit, videre tamen tenebras non potest, non absurde dicitur intellegi non posse stultitiam: nam nullas alias *mentis tenebras* nominamus. Nec iam illud movebit, quomodo stultitia possit non intellecta vitari. Ut enim oculis tenebras vitamus eo ipso quo nolumus non videre, sic quisquis volet vitare stultitiam, non eam conetur intellegere, sed ea quae possunt intellegi, per hanc se non intellegere doleat, eamque sibi esse praesentem, non quo ipsa magis intellegit, sed quo alia minus intellegit sentiat.

CAPUT IV

Quam homo perperam agit, an ordine agat. Mala in ordinem redacta faciunt ad decorem universi.

11. A. Sed ad ordinem redeamus, ut nobis aliquando reddatur

shared defeat with their patron without any fault of theirs, they would give in before you and be more cautious afterwards.

10. A. I have noticed that Trygetius was making noise wanting to say something in your defense. With your leave (for you are a newcomer to this debate) I will let him. They will argue their points without your support, and I shall hear them patiently as I had started doing in any case.

As Licentius wasn't there, Trygetius said:
T. – Call me a fool if you wish, and laugh at me. I do not think that we should call intellect the power by which we understand what foolishness is. The latter is in fact either the sole or the main cause of lack of understanding.
A. – I do not refuse to accept that outright, even though I am inclined to agree with Alypius. No one can rightly teach what he himself does not understand, and by such mental blindness he would inflict much damage on other minds. While paying a lot of attention, he was afraid of saying what you have just said, even though he had seen this same statement in some important book. Now considering bodily sense, which the soul makes use of after being informed by the mind, I am led to assert that no one can possibly see darkness. Therefore, understanding is to the mind what perceiving is to bodily sense. So if one is unable to see darkness despite one's eyes being open and clear, it is not absurd to say that it is impossible to understand foolishness, which is darkness of mind. It will not be difficult for me to explain how to avoid foolishness without understanding it. In the same way as we avoid darkness by the very fact that we want to see, anyone who wants to avoid foolishness should not try to understand what it is. He will regret what foolishness prevents him from understanding, not because he understands foolishness itself, but because it makes him understand less.

FOUR
Whether evil actions belong to order. Within order, evil contributes to the beauty of the universe.

11. A. – Back to order now, as Licentius may return any moment.

Licentius. Illud enim iam ex vobis requiro, utrum quaecumque agit stultus, ordine vobis agere videatur. Nam videte rogatio quos laqueos habeat. Si ordine dixeritis, ubi erit illa definitio: Ordo est quo Deus agit omnia quae sunt, si etiam stultus quae agit, agit ordine? Si autem ordo non est in iis quae aguntur ab stulto, erit aliquid quod ordo non teneat: neutrum autem vultis. Videte, quaeso, ne cuncta ipsius ordinis defensione turbetis.

Hic item Trygetius (nam ille alter adhuc omnino absens erat): **T.** – Facile est, inquit, huic quidem respondere complexioni tuae, sed me in praesentia similitudo deficit, qua sententiam meam video asseri illustrarique debere. Tamen dicam quod sentio; facies enim tu quod paulo ante fecisti. Non enim illa commemoratio tenebrarum ad id quod a me involutum prolatum erat, parum nobis attulit luminis. Namque omnis vita stultorum, quamvis per eos ipsos minime constans minimeque ordinata sit, per divinam tamen providentiam necessario rerum ordine includitur et quasi quibusdam locis illa ineffabili et sempiterna lege dispositis, nullo modo esse sinitur ubi esse non debet. Ita fit ut angusto animo ipsam solam quisque considerans, veluti magna repercussus foeditate aversetur. Si autem mentis oculos erigens atque diffundens, simul universa collustret nihil non ordinatum suisque semper veluti sedibus distinctum dispositumque reperiet.

12. A. – Quam magna, inquam, quam mira mihi per vos Deus ille atque ipse, ut magis magisque credere adducor, rerum nescio quis occultus ordo respondet! Nam ea dicitis quae nec quomodo dicantur non visa, nec quomodo ea videatis intellego; ita ea et vera et alta esse suspicor. Simile autem aliquod in istam sententiam tu fortasse unum requirebas. At mihi iam occurrunt innumerabilia, quae me ad consentiendum prorsus trahunt. Quid enim carnifice tetrius? Quid illo animo truculentius atque dirius? An inter ipsas leges locum necessarium tenet et in bene moderatae civitatis ordinem inseritur estque suo animo nocens, ordine autem alieno poena nocentium. Quid sordidius, quid inanius decoris et turpitudinis plenius meretricibus, lenonibus caeterisque hoc genus pestibus dici potest? Aufer meretrices de rebus humanis, turbaveris omnia libidinibus: constitue matronarum loco, labe ac dedecore dehonestaveris. Sic igitur hoc genus hominum per suos

Let me ask you whether you think that all foolish actions belong to order. But beware of the dilemma. If you say that they do, what do we make of the definition "Order is God's government of things that are," if even whatever a fool does belongs to that order? And if you deny that foolish actions belong to order, there are actions clearly left out of it. You would accept neither. Make sure, please, not to upset the very order you are trying to defend.

But Licentius was still away, so Trygetius said:

T. – It is an easy dilemma to undo. Right now, however, I cannot call to mind the right analogy with which to support and illustrate what I am going to say. Nevertheless I will give my impression, and you will do what you did a while ago with your analogy of the darkness. It succeeded in fact to clarify quite a bit what I had uttered rather confusedly. I say that the whole life of a fool, though running in fits and starts and in perennial disorder, is nevertheless inserted into the order of things by divine providence. God's ineffable and everlasting law has set aside a definite place for it, not allowing it to operate outside it. Should anyone then limit one's attention to the narrow reality of that life, he would feel utterly disgusted by it. But on raising the eyes of the mind to such heights as to survey the whole universe, he would find nothing out of order, each thing perfectly fitting in its own assigned place.

12. A. – Isn't it great and wonderful how that unfathomable order responds to me through you! It must be God himself, as I am more and more led to believe. I neither understand how you manage to say things that cannot be said without seeing them, nor how you actually see them. That is why I think they are true inspirations. You were looking for an analogy to illustrate your thoughts. I can think of countless ones, all leading me to agree with you. What is ghastlier than a savage and terrible public executioner? Yet he holds a necessary office in law, and is inserted in the social order of a well-governed state. His personal noxious character is ordered by others towards punishing other noxious characters. What is filthier, uglier, and more disgraceful than whores, procurers, and such-like plagues of humanity? Remove prostitutes from the social order, however, and lust will destroy it. Let them rise to the same status as married women, and you will

mores impurissimum vita, per ordinis leges conditione vilissimum. Nonne in corporibus animantium quaedam membra, si sola attendas, non possis attendere? Tamen et naturae ordo nec quia necessaria sunt, deesse voluit, nec quia indecora, eminere permisit. Quae tamen deformia suos locos tenendo, meliorem locum concessere melioribus. Quid nobis suavius, quod agro villaeque spectaculum congruentius fuit pugna illa conflictuque gallinaceorum gallorum, cuius superiore libro fecimus mentionem? Quid abiectius tamen deformitate subiecti vidimus? Et per ipsam tamen eiusdem certaminis perfectior pulchritudo provenerat.

13. Talia, credo, sunt omnia, sed oculos quaerunt. Soloecismos et barbarismos quos vocant, poetae adamaverunt; quae schemata et metaplasmos mutatis appellare nominibus quam manifesta vitia fugere maluerunt. Detrahe tamen ista carminibus, suavissima condimenta desiderabimus. Congere multa in unum locum, totum acre, putidum, rancidum, fastidibo. Transfer in liberam forensemque dictionem, quis non eam fugere atque in theatra se condere iubebit? Ordo igitur ea gubernans et moderans, nec apud se nimia nec ubilibet aliena esse patietur. Submissa quaedam impolitaeque simillima ipsos saltus ac venustos locos sese interponens illustrat oratio. Quae si sola sit, proiicis ut vilem: si autem desit, illa pulchra non prominent, non in suis quasi regionibus possessionibusque dominantur sibique ipsa propria luce obstant, totumque confundunt.

CAPUT V
Quomodo medendum errori credentium res nullo ordine geri

Magnae et hic debentur ordini gratiae. Mentientes conclusiones, aut irrepentes paulatim, vel minuendo vel addendo in assensionem falsitatis, quis non metuat?, quis non oderit? Saepe tamen in disputationibus certis et suis sedibus collocatae tantum

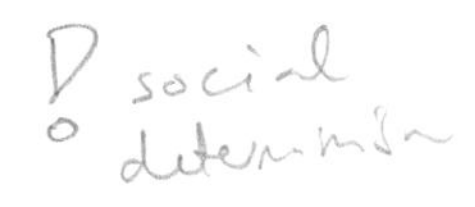

dishonor matrimony with an unseemly stain. This most unchaste lifestyle, therefore, places its practitioners at the very bottom of the social order. Equally, we are repelled by the shape of some animal organs on looking at them in isolation. But the order of nature wanted them where necessary, without however giving them undue prominence. Ugly as they are, they occupy their appointed place, leaving better places for better ones. Wasn't that fight between two cocks for the favor of their hens, mentioned in the previous book, a great sight? But, appropriately, we enjoyed it in a country setting. Wasn't the ruffled, vanquished cock a sorry sight? Yet it fitted within the perfection and overall beauty of the fight.

13. This is how things are, I think, but not how they appear. Poets love what other people call grammatical errors and foreign words; they prefer to call them "figures of speech" and "metaplasms" respectively rather than refrain from using what are clearly blunders. Remove such liberties from poetry, however, and it becomes spiceless food. Concentrate many of them in the same passage, and it will be sharp, pedantic, offensive. Use such words in ordinary speech, or in the market, and who wouldn't run off to the theatre on hearing them? Order governs and moderates them, neither tolerating too many nor avoiding them altogether. A rough sentence within a polished text makes the flight of fancy and the more ornate passage stand out. By itself it is cheap stuff, but without it, beautiful passages do not govern in their own realm as it were. They are obscured by their own brilliance, and all you get is confusion.

FIVE
Correcting the error of those who believe there is no order governing things

A. Thanks be to order, then. Who would not fear or hate conclusions which are either outright false or which introduce falsehood little by little by subtle addition or subtraction? But in a

valent, ut nescio quomodo per eas dulcescat ipsa deceptio. Nonne hic quoque ordo ipse laudabitur?

14. Iam in musica, in geometria, in astrorum motibus, in numerorum necessitatibus ordo ita dominatur ut si quis quasi eius fontem atque ipsum penetrale videre desideret, aut in his inveniat aut per haec eo sine ullo errore ducatur. Talis enim eruditio, si quis ea moderate utatur (nam nihil ibi quam nimium formidandum est), talem philosophiae militem nutrit vel etiam ducem ut ad summum illum modum, ultra quem requirere aliquid nec possit, nec debeat, nec cupiat, qua vult evolet atque perveniat multosque perducat. Unde iam, dum ipsis humanis rebus teneatur, sic eas despiciat cunctaque discernat, ut nullo modo eum moveat cur alius optet liberos habere nec habeat, alius nimia uxoris fecunditate torqueatur, egeat ille pecunia, qui largiri liberaliter multa paratus est, eique defossae incubet macer et scabiosus fenerator, ampla patrimonia luxuries dispergat atque diffundat, vix toto die lacrymans mendicus nummum impetret, alium honor extollat indignum, lucidi mores abscondantur in turba.

15. Haec et alia in hominum vita cogunt homines plerumque impie credere nullo nos ordine divinae providentiae gubernari. Alios autem pios et bonos atque splendido ingenio praeditos, qui neque nos deseri a summo Deo possunt in animum inducere et tamen rerum tanta quasi caligine atque commixtione turbati nullum ordinem vident, volentes sibi nudari abditissimas causas, errores suos saepe etiam carminibus conqueruntur. Qui si hoc solum interrogent, cur Itali semper serenas hiemes orent [Virgil, *Georgica* 1, 100] et item semper Getulia nostra misera sitiat, quis eis facile respondebit?, aut ubi apud nos indagabitur illius ordinis ulla suspicio? Ego autem, si quid meos monere possum, quantum mihi apparet quantumque sentio, censeo illos disciplinis omnibus erudiendos. Aliter quippe ista sic intelligi, ut luce clariora sint, nullo modo possunt. Si autem aut pigriores sunt aut aliis negotiis praeoccupati aut iam duri ad discendum, fidei sibi praesidia parent, quo illos vinculo ad sese trahat atque ab

properly conducted debate, and in their appointed place, they are often so valuable as to render deception itself pleasant. Does not even such an order deserve praise?

14. Take now music, geometry, the motion of the heavens, number theory. Order is so overpowering in these, that anyone seeking its source will either find it there, or will be led to it through them without error. This learning (in moderation, for nothing is more fearful than excess in these matters) forms excellent defenders and teachers of philosophy. They will attain themselves, and lead many to attain, that high standard beyond which nothing can or ought to be demanded or desired. From that vantage point, even in the thick of human affairs, they will size down and judge everything according to its real worth. Not strange for them that he who desires children doesn't have any, while another is distraught by his wife's excessive fertility. Or that he who is ready to give generously has no money, while the moneylender, himself half-starved and shabby, sleeps over a hole in the ground full of it. Or that riotous living destroys and scatters fortunes, while a tearful beggar scarcely gets a coin in a whole day; or that honors are heaped on scoundrels, while clean living passes unnoticed in the crowd.

15. These and other things of life lead many impiously to believe that there is no order of divine providence looking after us. Others are indeed pious, good, endowed with great minds but unable to bring themselves to accept that God may in any way abandon us. Lost in this fog and confusion, however, they fail to see any order in it. They seek the most extravagant causes, going so far as to bewail their own errors in song and verse. Were they to ask the single question, why do Italians always pray for fair weather, while our north of Africa thirsts for water, who could easily answer that? or where among us would this notion begin to be investigated? If I may say so to my own, I would encourage them to be instructed in all branches of learning. There is no other way to understand such things so as to become clearer than light. But if they be lazy, or overtaken by other worries, or just plain dull, let them have recourse to faith. God, who does not allow any believer

his horrendis et involutissimis malis liberet ille, qui neminem sibi per mysteria bene credentem perire permittit.

16. Duplex enim est via quam sequimur, cum rerum nos obscuritas movet, aut rationem, aut certe auctoritatem. Philosophia rationem promittit et vix paucissimos liberat, quos tamen non modo non contemnere illa mysteria, sed sola intellegere, ut intellegenda sunt, cogit. Nullumque aliud habet negotium, quae vera, et, ut ita dicam, germana philosophia est, quam ut doceat quod sit omnium rerum principium sine principio quantusque in eo maneat intellectus quidve inde in nostram salutem sine ulla degeneratione manaverit, quem unum Deum omnipotentem cum quo tripotentem, Patrem et Filium et Spiritum Sanctum, docent veneranda mysteria, quae fide sincera et inconcussa populos liberant, nec confuse, ut quidam, nec contumeliose, ut multi praedicant. Quantum autem illud sit, quod hoc etiam nostri generis corpus tantus propter nos Deus assumere agere dignatus est, quanto videtur vilius, tanto est clementia plenius et a quadam ingeniosorum superbia longe lateque remotius.

17. Anima vero unde originem ducat quidve hic agat, quantum distet a Deo, quid habeat proprium quod alternat in utramque naturam, quatenus moriatur et quomodo immortalis probetur, quam magni putatis esse ordinis, ut ista discantur? Magni omnino atque certi: de quo breviter, si tempus fuerit, post loquemur. Illud nunc a me accipiatis volo, si quis temere ac sine ordine disciplinarum in harum rerum cognitionem audet irruere, pro studioso illum curiosum, pro docto credulum, pro cauto incredulum fieri. Itaque mihi quod modo interroganti tam bene atque apte respondistis, et miror unde sit et cogor agnoscere. Videamus tamen quousque progredi vestra latens possit intentio. Iam nobis Licentii etiam verba reddantur, qui tam diu nescio qua cura occupatus, alienus ab hoc sermone fuit, ut eum ista non aliter quam eos qui non adsunt familiares nostros credam esse lecturum. Sed redi ad nos, quaeso, Licenti, atque hic totus fac ut adsis; tibi enim dico. Nam definitionem meam tu probasti, qua dictum est quid esse cum Deo, cum quo mentem sapientis manere immobilem me, quantum assequi valeo, docere voluisti.

in Him to perish, will by those mysteries call them to Himself and liberate them from such awful and confused evils.

16. There are two ways of getting through this darkness: either by reasoning or by certain authority. Philosophy does it by reasoning, but brings freedom to very few. It forces these few not only into not despising those mysteries, but to understand them insofar as possible. True and, so to speak, genuine philosophy can do no more than teach the First Principle of all things, itself without principle; what great knowledge is in it, and what riches issue from there for our immense benefit and without decrease on its part! This is none other than the one God almighty and thrice powerful, Father, Son, and Holy Spirit. These venerable mysteries liberate entire nations, neither by confusing them as some say, nor by doing violence to them as some others maintain. And how great, to cap it all, is the mystery of the Incarnation. For our sake God lowered himself to assuming a human body. The more demeaning such a thing appears, the more merciful and the farther away and out of the grasp of proud minds it is.

17. Don't you think it is a great matter of order to learn about the soul? It is indeed great to know its origin, its place from God in the hierarchy of being, in what sense it can be said to die and how it can be proved to be immortal. We shall briefly refer to it, time permitting. Now I want to impress on you one thing. Anyone who rushes into the learning of such disciplines rashly and disorderly becomes not a scholar but a searcher of vain curiosity, not learned but gullible, not cautious but faithless. That is why I must say I am astonished at how well you answered my questions just now, and wonder how you did it. Let us see how far your latent intellectual powers can go. Let us start by reading Licentius's words. I don't know what other worries have kept him away from this debate. I think that if he wants to be briefed he will have to read the matter as much as those friends of ours who are also absent. Come back to us, Licentius, and pay undivided attention from now on. It is to you I am talking. You proved my definition, and wanted to teach me, if I understand you, that the wise man's mind remains unmoved.

CAPUT VI
Mens sapientis immobilis

18. Sed illum me movet, quomodo cum iste sapiens quamdiu inter homines vivit in corpore esse non negetur, quo pacto fiat ut eius corpore huc atque illuc vagante, mens immobilis maneat. Isto enim modo potes dicere, cum movetur navis, homines qui in ea sunt non moveri, quamvis ab ipsis eam possideri gubernarique fateamur. Etenim si sola eam cogitatione regerent facerentque ire quo vellent, tamen, cum ea moveretur, non possent illi qui ibidem constituti sunt, non moveri.

L. – Non, ait Licentius, animus ita est in corpore ut corpus imperet animo.
A. – Neque hoc ego dico, inquam: sed etiam eques non ita est in equo ut ei equus imperet; et tamen, quamvis quo velit equum agat, equo moto moveatur necesse est.
L. – Potest, inquit, sedere ipse immobilis.
A. – Cogis nos, inquam, definire quid sit moveri: quod si potes, facias volo.
L. – Prorsus, inquit, maneat, quaeso, beneficium tuum, nam manet postulatio mea et ne me rursus interroges, utrum mihi definire placeat; quando id facere potuero, ipse profitebor.

Quae cum dicta essent, puer de domo cui dederamus id negotii, cucurrit ad nos et horam prandii esse nuntiavit.

Tum ego:
A. – Quid sit, inquam, moveri, non definire nos puer iste, sed ipsis oculis cogit ostendere. Eamus igitur et de isto loco in alium locum transeamus: nam nihil est aliud, nisi fallor, moveri.

Hic cum arrisissent, discessimus.

DISPUTATIO SECUNDA

19. At ubi refecimus corpora, quoniam caelum obduxerat nubes, solito loco in balneo consedimus. Atque ego:

A. – Concedis ergo, inquam, Licenti, nihil esse aliud motum quam de loco in locum transitum?

SIX
The wise man's mind is unmoved

18. What troubles me is how the wise man's mind remains unmoved while it cannot be denied that in real life he has a body moving here and there like everyone else's. You could say the same of a ship's crew, which can be said somehow not to move on the ship they own and control. Even if they were to control it by thought alone, directing it wherever they wished, since the ship moves, they could not possibly remain unmoved apart from it.

L. – No, the soul in its body is not meant to be governed by it.
A. – I didn't say that. A rider is not directed by the horse he rides; nevertheless, on reining the animal here and there, he necessarily moves with it.
L. – He can sit still though.
A. – Now you are forcing us to define what "to be moved" means. I would ask you to do it, if you can.
L. – Now it is your turn, as we have agreed. Don't ask me again whether I like to define things. When I am in a position to do so, I will tell you.

No sooner had we said that, than the boy in charge ran out towards us announcing lunch time. I said:
A. – This boy is forcing us not so much to define what "to be moved" means as to see it with our very eyes. Let's go from here to somewhere else: if I am not mistaken, that is what "to be moved" means.

They laughed, and we went.

SECOND DEBATE

19. After lunch the sky was dark with cloud, so we went indoors to our usual place. I started:

A. Licentius, would you agree that motion is nothing more than going from one place to another?

L. – Concedo, inquit.
A. – Concedis ergo, inquam, neminem in eo loco esse in quo non fuerat, et motum non fuisse?
L. – Non intellego, inquit.
A. – Si quid, inquam, in alio loco fuit dudum et nunc in alio est, motum esse concedis?
Assentiebatur.
A. – Ergo, inquam, posset alicuius sapientis vivum corpus hic modo nobiscum esse, ut animus hinc abesset?
L. – Posset, inquit.
A. – Etiamne, inquam, si nobiscum colloqueretur et nos aliquid doceret?
L. – Etiamsi, inquit, nos ipsam doceret sapientiam, non illum dicerem nobiscum esse, sed secum.
A. – Non igitur in corpore?, inquam.
L. – Non, inquit.
Cui ego:
A. – Corpus illud quod careret animo, nonne mortuum fatereris, cum ego vivum proposuerim?
L. – Nescio, inquit, quomodo explicem. Nam et corpus hominis vivum esse non posse video si animus in eo non sit, et non possum dicere, ubiubi sit corpus sapientis, non eius animum esse cum Deo.
A. – Ego, inquam, faciam ut hoc explices. Fortasse enim quia ubique Deus est, quoquo ierit sapiens, invenit Deum cum quo esse possit. Ita fit ut possimus et non negare illum de loco in locum transire, quod est moveri, et tamen semper esse cum Deo.
L. – Fateor, inquit, corpus illud de loco in locum transitum facere, sed mentem ipsam nego, cui nomen sapientis impositum est.

CAPUT VII
Quomodo ordo fuerit cum malum non esset

20. A. – Nunc interim tibi cedo, inquam, ne res obscurissima et diutius diligentiusque tractanda, impediat in praesentia propositum nostrum. Sed illud videamus, quoniam definitum est a nobis quid sit esse cum Deo, utrum scire possimus etiam quid sit esse

L. – I would.
A. – Do you also agree that nobody could be in a place where he was not before, without being moved there?
L. – I don't understand.
A. – If a thing was in a place before and now is in another, hasn't it been moved there?

He agreed.

A. – Therefore, could a wise man be with us right now in his living body, but not in his soul?
L. – He could.
A. – Even if he were talking to us, teaching us one thing or another?
L. – Even if he were to teach us wisdom itself, I would not deem him to be with us, but with himself.
A. – Not in the body?
L. – Not in the body.
A. – Were I to affirm that a soulless body was alive, wouldn't you maintain it was dead?
L. – I don't know how to explain. Clearly I could not maintain that a human soulless body was alive, and yet I am unable to affirm, in whichever place the body of a wise man might be, that his soul was not with God.
A. – I will help you to explain that. God is everywhere. Perhaps then, wherever a wise man might go, there he finds God with whom he might be. That is why we can assert both his going from place to place, which is to be moved, and his always being with God.
L. – I agree that his body moves from place to place, but I deny it of his mind, if he really deserves to be called wise.

SEVEN
What kind of order there would be in the absence of evil

20. **A.** – I grant that for the time being, to avoid getting into a most obscure matter that deserves close scrutiny. It would stop us in our tracks if we did. Let us go back instead to our defining "being with God," to see whether we can deduce what "being

sine Deo, quamvis iam manifestum esse arbitror. Nam credo videri tibi eos qui cum Deo non sunt esse sine Deo.
L. – Si possent, inquit, mihi verba suppetere, dicerem fortasse quod tibi non displiceret. Sed peto perferas infantiam meam resque ipsas, ut te decet, veloci mente praeripias. Nam isti nec cum Deo mihi videntur esse et a Deo tamen haberi. Itaque non possum eos sine Deo esse dicere quos Deus habet. Cum Deo item non dico, quia ipsi non habent Deum. Siquidem Deum habere, iam inter nos pridem in sermone illo quem die natali tuo iucundissimum habuimus, placuit nihil aliud esse quam Deo perfrui. Sed fateor me formidare ista contraria, quomodo quisque nec sine Deo sit nec cum Deo.

21. A. – Non te moveant ista, inquam. Nam ubi res convenit, quis non verba contemnat? Quare iam ad illam tandem ordinis definitionem redeamus. Nam ordinem esse dixisti quo Deus agit omnia. Nihil autem, ut video, non agit Deus: nam inde visum tibi est nihil praeter ordinem posse inveniri.
L. – Manet, inquit, sententia mea: sed iam video quid sis dicturus, utrum Deus agat quae non bene agi confitemur.
A. – Optime, inquam; prorsus oculum in mentem iniecisti. Sed ut vidisti quid essem dicturus, ita peto videas quid respondendum sit.
Atque ille nutans capite atque humeris:
L. – Turbamur, inquit.
Et huic forte quaestioni mater supervenerat. Atque ille post aliquantulum silentium petiit ut a me hoc ipsum rursus interrogaretur. Cui loco superius a Trygetio fuisse responsum non omnino animadverterat. Tum ego:
A. – Quid, inquam, vel cur tibi repetam? "Actum, aiunt, ne agas" [Terence, *Phormio* 419]. Quare moneo potius ut ea quae supra dicta sunt vel legere cures si audire nequivisti. Quam quidem absentiam a sermone nostro animi tui non aegre tuli diuque ita esse pertuli, ut neque illa impedirem quae tecum intentus remotusque a nobis pro te agebas, et ea persequerer quae te amittere stilus iste non sineret.

22. Nunc illud quaero quod nondum discutere diligenti ratione

without God" might mean. I see it clearly myself, but I have the impression that you think "not being with God" equivalent to "being without God."

L. – If the right words came to mind, what I said would perhaps sound nice to you. But I ask you to put up with my inability to express myself. Your sharp mind will grasp such things, as is usual with you. I don't see such people being with God; nevertheless I see them possessed by God. Therefore I am unable to affirm that those whom God possesses are not with Him. But neither can I affirm that they be with God, for it is they who do not have God. Because, during the conversation held on your most happy birthday, we agreed that "to be with God" means to enjoy His presence. I must admit that these paradoxes, like being and not being with God, rather frighten me.

21. A. – Forget that. Agreement on the matter renders words irrelevant. Let us return to our definition of order. You said that order is God's action on everything. If I understand, there is nothing outside that action, and that's why you are of the opinion that nothing is to be found outside order.

L. – I still think so. But I can see what you are going to say: that things badly done are also God's action.

A. – Yes. You have read my thoughts. As good as you are at mind reading, let us see if you also get the counter-objection.

He shook his head and shrugged his shoulders:

L. – I am confused, he admitted.

My mother had arrived at that very moment. He paused a little and then asked me to question him again. He was completely unaware that Trygetius had already solved the question. I said:

A. – What should I repeat, and why? "Don't do what has already been done," Terentius warns. I would ask you to read the proceedings of what has already been discussed, since you were not here to hear it yourself. I did not mind your being absent for so long during our conversation. I did not wish to prevent you from doing whatever has kept you away from us, but I pursued the argument, since its written record would preserve it for your attention.

22. I want now to talk about something that has not yet come to

tentavimus. Nam ut primum nobis istam de ordine quaestionem nescio quis ordo peperit, memini te dixisse hanc esse iustitiam Dei, quae separat inter bonos et malos et sua cuique tribuit. Nam ulla est, quantum sentio, manifestior iustitiae definitio: itaque respondeas velim utrum tibi videatur aliquando Deum non fuisse iustum.

L. – Numquam, inquit.

A. – Si ergo semper, inquam, Deus iustus, semper bonum et malum fuerunt.

M. – Prorsus, inquit mater, nihil aliud video quod sequatur. Non enim iudicium Dei fuit ullum quando malum non fuit, nec, si aliquando bonis et malis sua cuique non tribuit, potest videri iustus fuisse.

Cui Licentius:

L. – Ergo dicendum nobis censes, inquit, semper malum fuisse.

M. – Non audeo, inquit illa, hoc dicere.

A. – Quid ergo dicemus?, inquam. Si Deus ideo iustus est, quia iudicat inter bonos et malos, quando non erat malum, non erat iustus.

Hic illis tacentibus, animadverti Trygetium respondere velle atque permisi. At ille:

T. – Prorsus, inquit, erat Deus iustus. Poterat enim bonum malumque secernere, si exstitisset, et ex ipso quo poterat iustus erat. Non enim, cum dicimus Ciceronem prudenter investigasse coniurationem Catilinae, temperanter nullo corruptum fuisse praemio quo parceret malis, iuste illos summo supplicio senatus auctoritate mactasse, fortiter sustinuisse omnia tela inimicorum et molem, ut ipse dixit, invidiae [Cicero, *In Catilinam* 1, 9, 23], non in eo fuissent virtutes istae, nisi Catilina reipublicae tantam perniciem comparasset. Virtus enim per seipsam, non per aliquod huiusmodi opus consideranda est et in homine, quanto magis in Deo?, si tamen in angustiis rerum atque verborum componere illis ista quoquo modo permittitur. Nam, ut intellegamus quia Deus semper iustus fuit, quando exstitit malum quod a bono seiungeret, nihil distulit sua cuique tribuere: non enim tunc ei erat discenda iustitia, sed tunc ea utendum, quam semper habuit.

our attention. When an unexpected order of things led us into discussing order itself, I remember your affirming that God's justice consists in separating the good from the evil ones, giving everyone his due. There is no clearer definition of justice as I see it: but answer now whether you think that God was not just at some time or other.
L. – Never.
A. – Ergo, if God was always just, good and evil have always been around.

My mother intervened:
M. – Of course. I don't see how anything else can follow. There was no judgment of God in the absence of evil, nor could He be said to be just unless He gave their due to both good and evil.

L. – In your opinion, then, we should say that evil has always been around.
M. – Not for me to dare say such a thing.
L. – What then?
A. – If for God to be just it is necessary that he judge between good and evil, if there was no evil there would be no justice of God.

In the general silence I noticed that Trygetius wanted to say something. I gave him leave.
T. – God was certainly always just. He could have separated good and evil, if the latter existed, and by this very faculty he has always been just. Take Catilina's conspiracy, for instance. We say that Cicero exercised prudence in investigating it, temperance in not allowing himself to be bribed into forgiving the evildoers, justice in having them condemned to death by the Senate, and fortitude in bearing both the blows of his enemies and those of envy as he himself said. We don't say that he would not have had these virtues without Catilina's attempt at bringing harm to the state. So if human virtue is to be considered in itself and not in the set of circumstances of its practice, how much more divine virtue? And I leave out the inadequacy of our language for comparing one reality with another in any way. Let us therefore understand that God has always been just. When evil appeared, separating itself from good, God at once repaid that act of separation. He didn't have to learn what justice was, but to administer what he always had.

23. Quod cum et Licentius et mater in tanta necessitate approbassent:

A. – Quid, inquam, dicis, Licenti? Ubi est quod tam magnopere asseruisti, nihil praeter ordinem fieri? Quod enim factum est ut malum nasceretur, non utique Dei ordine factum est, sed cum esset natum, Dei ordine inclusum est. Et ille admirans et moleste ferens quod tam repente bona causa esset lapsa de manibus:
L. – Prorsus, inquit, ex illo dico coepisse ordinem ex quo malum esse coepit.
A. – Ergo, inquam, ut esset ipsum malum, non ordine factum est, si postquam malum ortum est ordo esse coepit. Semper erat ordo apud Deum et aut semper fuit nihil quod dicitur malum; aut si aliquando invenitur coepisse, quia ordo ipse aut bonum est aut ex bono est, nunquam aliquid sine ordine fuit nec erit aliquando. Quamvis et nescio quid potius occurrit, sed illa consuetudine oblivionis elapsum est: quod credo ordine contigisse pro merito vel gradu vel ordine vitae.
L. – Nescio quomodo mihi, inquit, effugit quam nunc sperno sententiam: non enim debui dicere postquam malum natum est coepisse ordinem: sed ut illa iustitia, de qua Trygetius disseruit, ita et ordinem fuisse apud Deum, sed ad usum non venisse, nisi postquam mala esse coeperunt.
A. – Eodem, inquam, relaberis; illud enim, quod minime vis, inconcussum manet: nam sive apud Deum fuit ordo, sive ex illo tempore esse coepit, ex quo etiam malum, tamen malum illud praeter ordinem natum est. Quod si concedis, fateris aliquid praeter ordinem posse fieri, quod causam tuam debilitat ac detruncat: si autem non concedis, incipit Dei ordine natum malum videri et malorum auctorem Deum fateberis, quo sacrilegio mihi detestabilius nihil occurrit.

Quod cum sive non intellegenti sive dissimulanti se intellexisse, versarem saepius et evolverem, nihil habuit quod diceret et se silentio dedit. Tum mater:
M. – Ego, inquit, non puto nihil potuisse praeter Dei ordinem fieri, quia ipsum malum quod natum est nullo modo Dei ordine natum est, sed illa iustitia id inordinatum esse non sivit et in sibi meritum ordinem redegit et compulit.

23. Licentius and my mother approved in agreement.

A. – What are you saying, Licentius? Were you not asserting before that there is nothing outside order? Whatever caused evil to come into being was not part of God's order. On being born, evil was incorporated into God's order.

He seemed surprised and troubled at seeing such a good argument suddenly slip from his hands.

L. – That's what I maintain. Order began the moment evil came into being.

A. – Therefore evil could not come out of order, if order began after evil came into being. Order, however, was always with God. As to this non-entity we call evil, it either always was, or it began at some stage. And since order itself is either good or proceeds from good, there was never anything outside order nor will there ever be. Although something may happen, and afterwards escape my mind as usual, I would still accept that this very phenomenon would have happened because of a certain order: a reason of its own, perhaps, or its being a necessary step in life, or being part of the order of life itself.

L. – I don't know how I said something I now regret. I should not have said that order began after evil appeared, but that justice, as Trygetius well said, was in God as much as order was, but it was not done until evils began.

A. – There you are again. The conclusion you dislike still stands: whether order was always in God, or it began at the time when evil did, evil was born outside of order. If you grant that, you admit that something may happen outside order, so weakening and mutilating your argument; and if you don't, you admit that evil appears to begin within God's order, turning God into the author of evil. A detestable sacrilege if ever there was one.

Despite my explanations from different vantage points, either he did not understand or pretended not to, and kept quiet. Mother intervened:

M. – I reject the notion that nothing at all can happen outside God's order. The very evil that began did not do so from within God's order, but God's justice did not allow it to stay out of that order, but reduced and compelled it to become part of it.

24. Hic ego cum omnes cernerem studiosissime ac pro suis quemque viribus Deum quaerere, sed ipsum de quo agebamus ordinem non tenere quo ad illius ineffabilis maiestatis intelligentiam pervenitur:

A. – Oro vos, inquam, si ut video multum diligitis ordinem, ne nos praeposteros et inordinatos esse patiamini. quamquam enim occultissima ratio se demonstraturam polliceatur nihil praeter divinum ordinem fieri, tamen si quempiam ludimagistrum audiremus conantem docere puerum syllabas, quem prius litteras nemo docuisset, non dico ridendum tamquam stultum, sed vinciendum tamquam furiosum putaremus, non ob aliud, opinor, nisi quod docendi ordinem non teneret. At multa talia et imperitos, quae a doctis reprehendantur ac derideantur, et dementes homines, quae nec stultorum iudicium fugiunt, facere nemo ambigit: et tamen etiam ista omnia quae fatemur esse perversa, non esse praeter divinum ordinem, alta quaedam et a multitudinis vel suspicione remotissima disciplina, se ita studiosis et Deum atque animas tantum amantibus animis manifestaturam esse promittit ut non nobis summae numerorum possint esse certiores.

CAPUT VIII
Traduntur primum adolescentibus praecepta vitae, tum ordo eruditionis

25. A. Haec autem disciplina ista Dei lex est, quae apud eum fixa et inconcussa semper manens, in sapientes animas quasi transcribitur, ut tanto se sciant vivere melius tantoque sublimius, quanto et perfectius eam contemplantur intelligendo, et vivendo custodiunt diligentius. Haec igitur disciplina eis qui illam nosse desiderant, simul geminum ordinem sequi iubet, cuius una pars vitae, altera eruditionis est.

Adolescentibus ergo studiosis eius ita vivendum est ut a venereis rebus, ab illecebris ventris et gutturis, ab immodesto corporis cultu et ornatu, ab inanibus negotiis ludorum, a torpore somni atque pigritiae, ab aemulatione, obtrectatione, invidentia, ab honorum potestatumque ambitionibus, ab ipsius etiam laudis immodica cupiditate se abstineant. Amorem autem pecuniae

24. Here I could see that all were seeking God to the best of their abilities, but lacked the order by which one is led to the understanding of His ineffable majesty. So I said:

A. – If, as I see, you love order that much, please make sure not to be in any way perverted and disorderly. It is true that we all harbor in the back of our minds the idea that nothing happens outside divine order. Nevertheless, should we hear a schoolmaster teaching a boy the syllables before anyone had taught him the alphabet, we would not so much laugh at him for being a fool, as bind him for being a madman. What else is not to follow the teaching order? No one contends that the ignorant do such things, for which those in the know scold and laugh at them, and madmen do things for which they do not even escape the judgment of fools. But even all these things that we call perverted are not outside the divine order. There is a branch of higher learning far, far above the grasp of the crowd, which opens vistas to those who intend to study God and the soul. It promises to expound such truths to us as to give a certainty far superior to that afforded by mathematical truth.

EIGHT

Instructions for the youth: how to live and how to learn in order

25. A. – This discipline is none other than God's own law. Ever the same, fixed and unchangeable, it gets transcribed, as it were, in wise souls. They will know how to live and at what high level, in direct proportion to how perfectly they contemplate it and how diligently they keep it in their lives. To those who wish to know it, this discipline imposes a double order: of life and of learning.

You, its youthful students, must begin by abstaining from sex, from the enticement of gluttony and drunkenness, the immodest undue care of body and dress, vain sports and games, the torpor of excess sleep and laziness, ill-natured rivalry, detraction, envy, ambition for office and power, down to excessive desire for simple praise. Know that the love of money is the certain ruin of all your hopes. Do nothing willy-nilly, or rashly. Do not get angry at the faults of friends and acquaintances, and if you do, swallow

totius suae spei certissimum venenum esse credant. Nihil enerviter faciant, nihil audaciter. In peccatis autem suorum vel pellant omnino iram, vel ita frenent ut sit pulsae similis. Neminem oderint. Nulla vitia non curare velint. Magnopere observent cum vindicant ne nimium sit, cum ignoscunt, ne parum. Nihil puniant quod non valeat ad melius, nihil indulgeant quod vertat in peius. Suos putent omnes, in quos sibi potestas data fuerit. Ita serviant ut eis dominari pudeat, ita dominentur ut eis servire delectet. In alienorum autem peccatis molesti non sint invito. Inimicitias vitent cautissime, ferant aequissime, finiant citissime. In omni vero contractu atque conversatione cum hominibus, satis est servare unum hoc vulgare proverbium: Nemini faciant quod pati nolunt. Rempublicam nolint administrare, nisi perfecti. Perfici autem vel intra aetatem senatoriam festinent, vel certe intra iuventutem. Sed quisquis sero in ista se converterit, non arbitretur nihil sibi esse praeceptum: nam ista utique facilius decocta aetate servabit. In omni autem vita, loco, tempore, amicos aut habeant aut habere instent. Obsequantur dignis etiam non hoc exspectantibus. Superbos minus curent, minime sint. Apte congruenterque vivant. Deum colant, cogitent, quaerant, fide, spe, caritate subnixi. Optent tranquillitatem atque certum cursum studiis suis, omniumque sociorum, et sibi quibusque possunt mentem bonam pacatamque vitam.

CAPUT IX
Ad discendum auctoritate ducimur et ratione

26. Sequitur ut dicam quomodo studiosi erudiri debeant, qui sicut dictum est vivere instituerunt. At discendum item necessario dupliciter ducimur, auctoritate atque ratione. Tempore auctoritas, re autem ratio prior est. Aliud est enim quod in agendo anteponitur, aliud quod pluris in appetendo aestimatur. Itaque, quamquam bonorum auctoritas imperitae multitudini videatur esse salubrior, ratio vero aptior eruditis, tamen quia nullus hominum nisi ex imperito peritus fit, nullus autem imperitus novit qualem se debeat praebere docentibus et quali vita esse docilis possit, evenit ut

your anger, so as not to show it. Refrain from hating anyone. Do not fall into vice of any kind. Do not take excessive vengeance when punishing, or be mean in forgiving. Above all do not punish unless it is for the sake of improvement, and don't be lenient on anyone who might get worse by it. Treat those under your authority as if they belonged to your own family. Serve to the extent of embarrassment those who give you orders, and exercise authority so as to make it a delight to obey you. Don't be unwilling to correct other people's faults. Avoid enmity most cautiously, bear it most equitably, bring it to an end as fast as possible. In all kinds of dealings with people, keep in mind the popular saying: Do not do unto others what you do not wish to be done unto you. Do not aspire to public office before time. Attain the necessary maturity for it before the twenty-fifth year, better if earlier. Should you arrive late to the study of this discipline, do not think yourself exempt from the foregoing advice: it is easier to assimilate it in mature age. Have friends or seek to have them in any circumstance of life, anywhere and at any time. Defer to worthy persons, even though they may not desire it. Ignore the proud, and above all don't be proud yourself. Live in an orderly and harmonious way. Worship, think about and love God with the support of faith, hope, and love. Pursue peace and due order in your studies, those of your friends and whoever else has talent, with a view to a good mind and a quiet life.

NINE
We learn by authority and reason

26. A. – Next I will explain how those students should learn who have decided so to live. We are led to learning by a twofold path: *authority* and *reason*. Authority comes first in time, reason in the reality of things. What gets done first is one thing, and what is utmost in one's intention entirely another. And so the uninstructed crowd sets store by the authority of good people, while the learned prefer reason. The point is, however, that no one progresses from ignorance to knowledge automatically, and the ignorant have no idea of how docile they have to be both to their teachers and to a disciplined

omnibus bona magna et occulta discere cupientibus non aperiat nisi auctoritas ianuam.

Quam quisque ingressus sine ulla dubitatione vitae optimae praecepta sectatur, per quae cum docilis factus fuerit, tum demum discet et quanta ratione praedita sint ea ipsa quae secutus est ante rationem, et quid sit ipsa ratio quam post auctoritatis cunabula firmus et idoneus iam sequitur atque comprehendit et quid intellectus, in quo universa sunt, vel ipse potius universa, et quid praeter universa universorum principium. Ad quam cognitionem in hac vita pervenire pauci, ultra quam vero etiam post hanc vitam nemo progredi potest.

Qui autem sola auctoritate contenti bonis tantum moribus rectisque votis constanter operam dederint, aut contemnentes, aut non valentes disciplinis liberalibus atque optimis erudiri, beatos eos quidem, cum inter homines vivunt, nescio quomodo appellem; tamen inconcusse credo mox ut hoc corpus reliquerint, eos quo bene magis minusve vixerunt, eo facilius aut difficilius liberari.

27. Auctoritas autem partim divina est, partim humana: sed vera, firma, summa ea est quae divina nominatur. In qua metuenda est aeriorum animalium mira fallacia, quae per rerum ad istos sensus corporis pertinentium quasdam divinationes nonnullasque potentias, decipere animas facillime consuerunt, aut periturarum fortunarum curiosas, aut fragilium cupidas potestatum, aut inanium formidolosas miraculorum.

Illa ergo auctoritas divina dicenda est, quae non solum in sensibilibus signis transcendit omnem humanam facultatem, sed et ipsum hominem agens ostendit ei quousque se propter ipsum depresserit; et non teneri sensibus, quibus videntur illa miranda, sed ad intellectum iubet evolare, simul demonstrans et quanta hic possit et cur haec faciat et quam parvi pendat. Doceat enim oportet et factis potestatem suam et humilitate clementiam et praeceptione naturam, quae omnia sacris quibus initiamur, secretius firmiusque traduntur, in quibus bonorum vita facillime, non disputationum ambagibus sed mysteriorum auctoritate purgatur.

lifestyle. Therefore it is authority alone that opens the gates of learning to those eagerly wishing to know good, great, and hidden truths.

Those who unhesitatingly enter and follow the precepts of a good life acquire the virtue of docility. Only then do they appreciate how reasonable were the notions they learned before understanding them. They also follow and understand reason itself firmly and surely, after leaving the cradle of authority. They understand how the entire universe can fit into the intellect, which becomes itself a universe, as it were. And they attain that supreme principle of all things beyond the universe. Few indeed are those who climb up to this kind of knowledge in this life, and even in the next no one can go beyond it.

There are some, however, who have no use for the liberal arts and for higher learning, which they either despise or have no talent for. Nevertheless they live a clean life of upright desires. I don't know whether to call such people happy during this life; I believe, nevertheless, that no sooner do they leave this body of ours, than they will get liberated in direct proportion to the effort they have put into living a good life.

27. Authority is partly divine and partly human. The former is the truest, firmest, and supreme. In such matters we ought to fear the devil's uncanny power of deception through divination of material things perceived by the senses. By some power they possess they have succeeded, with the utmost ease, in deceiving souls seeking vain success, lusting after perishable power, or easily frightened by vain wonders.

What deserves to be called divine is the authority which not only acts beyond all human power with miracles perceived by the senses, but, acting on man himself, shows him how far down he has fallen by his own fault. It further commands him not to stick to the level of the senses, to which all those vain things seem marvelous, but to soar to the level of the intellect, showing what great things it can do there, why, and how little it values them. It must needs teach its power by deeds, its mercy by coming down so low, its nature by command. We are taught all that in the sacred rites of initiation. It is there that the good purify their lives most easily, not by beating around the bush of debate, but by the authority of mystery.

Humana vero auctoritas plerumque fallit: in eis tamen iure videtur excellere, qui quantum imperitorum sensus capit, multa dant indicia doctrinarum suarum et non vivunt aliter quam vivendum esse praecipiunt. Quibus si aliqua etiam fortunae munera accesserint, quorum appareant usu magni contemptuque maiores, difficillimum omnino est ut eis quisque vivendi praecepta dantibus credens, recte vituperetur.

CAPUT X
Vita praecepta pauci assequuntur

Hic Alypius:
28. Al. – Permagna, inquit, vitae imago abs te ante oculos nostros, cum plene, tum breviter constituta est; cui quamvis quotidianis praeceptis tuis inhiemus, tamen nos hodie cupidiores flagrantioresque reddidisti. Ad quam, si fieri posset, non solum nos, verum etiam cunctos homines iam pervenire et eidem inhaerere cuperem, ut haec auditu mirabilia, ita essent imitatione facilia. Nam nescio quomodo, quod utinam vel a nobis procul absit, animus humanus dum haec audiendo caelestia, divina ac prorsus vera esse proclamet, in appetendo aliter se gerit, ut mihi verissimum videatur aut divinos homines, aut non sine divina ope sic vivere.
Cui ego:
A. – Haec praecepta vivendi, quae tibi, ut semper, plurimum placent, Alypi, quamvis hic meis verbis pro tempore expressa sint, non tamen a me inventa esse optime scis. His enim magnorum hominum et paene divinorum libri plenissimi sunt: quod non propter te dicendum mihi putavi, sed propter istos adolescentes, ne in eis quasi auctoritatem meam iure contemnant. Nam mihi omnino illos nolo credere, nisi docenti rationemque reddenti, propter quos pro rerum magnitudine concitandos etiam te arbitror istum interposuisse sermonem. Non enim tibi sunt ad sequendum ista difficilia, quae tanta rapuisti aviditate tantoque in ea naturae admirabilis impetu ingressus es, ut ego tibi verborum, tu mihi rerum magister effectus sis. Non enim est modo ulla causa mentiendi aut saltem occasio, nam neque te falsa tua laude studiosiorem

Human authority, on the other hand, often deceives. It would seem right that those who are the best at this game should give abundant proofs of their doctrines and live according to them. Should they further have achieved material wealth, using it in practice and appearing to despise it in theory, it would be very difficult to blame those who give credit to the doctrines broadcast by such men.

TEN
Few follow the norms of right living

28. Al. – What an overall view of life have you placed before our eyes! It was concise, yet complete. Although your daily teachings lead us to desire it, today you have fanned our desires to red heat. I wish it were possible that not only we, but everyone arrived at such a lifestyle and held onto it. What sounds so great in theory would thus easily be put into practice by imitation. I don't know how though, but everyone – not us, God forbid – on hearing such things does not hesitate in proclaiming them heavenly, divine, and absolutely true. In practice, however, they do exactly the opposite. What I think absolutely true is that you need divinized humans, or divine help to lead such an ideal lifestyle.
A. – You know very well, Alypius, that these norms of right living which you have always liked came dressed in my words in the right context, but they are by no means my invention. The books of great and saintly men are full of such. I did not speak for your sake, but for these young men here, that they may not rightly despise these precepts as if they were mine. I have no wish that they should believe my words, unless I give reasons. What you have just said is, I think, an excellent means to stir their minds towards a matter of such a great importance. You, in fact, do not find it difficult to practice such things. You grasped them with such eagerness and entered into them with such determination, that you have been my master by example, unlike me who has been yours by word of mouth only. This is neither cause nor occasion for flattery. I know you are not going to become more devoted

fieri puto, et ii adsunt qui utrumque noverunt, et ei sermo iste mittetur, cui nostrum nullus ignotus est.

29. Bonos autem viros deditosque optimis moribus, si non aliter sentis atque dixisti, pauciores te arbitror esse credere quam mihi probabile est, sed multi penitus latent te. Item multorum non latentium, ea ipsa quae mira sunt latent: in animo enim sunt ista, qui neque sensu accipi potest et plerumque dum congruere vult vitiosorum hominum colloquiis, ea dicit quae aut probare aut appetere videatur. Multa etiam facit non libenter, propter autem vitandum odium hominum aut ineptiam fugiendam, quod nos audientes aut videntes difficile aliter existimamus quam sensus iste renuntiat. Eoque fit ut multos non tales esse credamus, quales et se ipsi et eos suos familiares noverunt. Quod tibi ex amicorum nostrorum quibusdam magnis animi bonis, quae nos soli scimus, persuadeas velim. Nam error iste non minima hac causa nititur quod non pauci se subito ad bonam vitam miramque convertunt, et donec aliquibus clarioribus factis innotescant, quales erant esse creduntur. Nam ne longius abeam, quis istos adolescentes, qui antea noverat, facile credat tam studiose magna quaerere, tantas repente in hac aetate indixisse inimicitias voluptatibus? Ergo hanc opinionem pellamus ex animo; nam et illud divinum auxilium, quod, ut decebat, religiose in ultimo sermonis tui posuisti, latius quam nonnulli opinantur officium clementiae suae per universos populos agit. Sed ad disputationis nostrae, si placet, ordinem redeamus et quoniam de auctoritate satis dictum est, videamus quid sibi ratio velit.

CAPUT XI
Ratio quid, et huius in sensibilibus vestigia. Ut differunt rationale et rationabile.

30. Ratio est mentis motio, ea quae discuntur distinguendi et connectendi potens, qua duce uti ad Deum intellegendum, vel ipsam quae aut in nobis aut usquequaque est animam, rarissimum omnino genus hominum potest, non ob aliud, nisi quia in istorum

to your studies out of false praise. Those present know both of us, and this paper will be sent to Zenobius, who knows everybody here.

29. If you meant what you said, there are far fewer good men with clean lives according to you than to me. But many are wholly out of sight. Those who are not, keep out of sight their most admirable qualities, those of their souls. The senses cannot perceive such qualities. What is more, when such a person holds intercourse with others given to vice, he says things that he appears either to approve of or to desire. He also does many things against his better judgment, either to avoid being hated by others, or to run away from their foolishness. On hearing of or seeing such behavior, it is difficult for us to judge otherwise than the senses suggest. As a result we fail to appreciate the quality of many of these people in their own judgment and that of their friends and acquaintances. To convince you of this, just think of the great qualities of some of our friends, equalities that are known to us alone. Not the least cause of this error is the sudden conversion of some of them. Until such a time as the fact becomes well known, they are still believed to be their old selves. Not to go too far: who, having previously been acquainted with these young men here, would accept now that they so suddenly and at such youthful age had acquired such a taste for great things as to declare war on worldly pleasure? Let us rid ourselves of this opinion then. God's help, which you piously mentioned towards the end of your intervention, routinely exercises mercy on people of all sorts, and to a wider extent than many believe. But let us go back to the order of topics in our debate. About authority we have said enough. Let us now tackle reason.

ELEVEN
Reason and its traces in what the senses perceive. What is rational and what is reasonable.

30. Reason is a mental operation with the power to distinguish between, and to connect, things we learn. Few extraordinary men have the ability to let themselves be guided by it into knowing God and the soul, their own or other people's. This is because

sensuum negotia progresso redire in semetipsum cuique difficile est. Itaque cum in rebus ipsis fallacibus ratione totum agere homines moliantur, quid sit ipsa ratio et qualis sit nisi perpauci prorsus ignorant. Mirum videtur, sed tamen se ita res habet. Satis est hoc dixisse in praesentia: nam si vobis rem tantam sicut intellegenda est nunc ostendere cupiam, tam ineptus sim quam arrogans, si vel me illam iam percepisse profitear. Tamen quantum dignata est in res quae nobis notae videntur procedere, indagemus eam, si possumus interim, prout susceptus sermo desiderat.

31. Ad primum videamus ubi hoc verbum, quod *ratio* vocatur, frequentari solet; nam illud nos movere maxime debet, quod ipse homo a veteribus sapientibus ita definitus est: Homo est animal rationale mortale [Aristotle, *Topica 132b2;* also Cicero, *Lucullus* 7, 21]. Hic genere posito quod *animal* dictum est, videmus additas duas differentias, quibus credo admonendus erat homo et quo sibi redeundum esset et unde fugiendum. Nam ut progressus animae usque ad mortalia lapsus est, ita regressus esse in rationem debet. Uno verbo a bestiis, quod rationale; et alio a divinis separatur quod mortale dicitur. Illud igitur nisi tenuerit, bestia erit; hinc nisi se averterit, divina non erit. Sed quoniam solent doctissimi viri quid inter *rationale* et *rationabile* intersit acute subtiliterque discernere, nullo modo est, ad id quod instituimus, neglegendum: nam *rationale* esse dixerunt quod ratione uteretur vel uti posset, *rationabile* autem, quod ratione factum esse aut dictum. Itaque has balneas *rationabiles* possumus dicere nostrumque sermonem, *rationales* autem vel illum qui has fecit, vel nos qui loquimur. Ergo procedit ratio ab anima rationali, scilicet in ea quae vel fiunt rationabilia vel dicuntur.

32. Duo ergo video, in quibus potentia visque rationis possit ipsis etiam sensibus admoveri: opera hominum quae videntur et verba quae audiuntur. In utroque autem utitur mens gemino nuntio pro corporis necessitate: uno qui oculorum est, altero qui aurium. Itaque, cum aliquid videmus congruentibus sibi partibus figuratum, non absurde dicimus rationabiliter apparere. Itemque, cum aliquid bene concinere audimus, non dubitamus dicere quod

those who have gone a long way in the pursuit of sense reality find it extremely difficult to enter into themselves. And, as most people strive to use reason even in deception and falsehood, with a few exceptions they have no idea of the nature of reason itself and of its qualities. Strange to relate, but true. Enough said, for if I were to launch into explaining such an important matter as this, I would be both inept and arrogant for avowing an understanding that I lack. Nevertheless, since it has appeared here and there in the things we have already considered, let us have a look at it if we can, according to the trend of our conversation.

31. First, let us see the most common usage of this term "reason." It is most important for us to recall that ancient philosophers defined man as an animal both rational and mortal. Having fitted man into the genus "animal," they added two differences, which were perhaps meant, as I understand it, to point out to man himself where to return to and what to flee from. In fact the soul's progress has been downwards to perishable realities, so its return must be upwards towards reason. The term "rational" sets him aside from the beasts, and the term "mortal" from God. Should he lose rationality, he would be no more than a beast, and unless he ceased to be such, he could not be divinized. Let us not neglect the fact that most learned men debated the difference between "rational" and "reasonable": it fits into what we have been discussing so far. They used the term "rational" for beings that did or could use reason, and "reasonable" for what is said or done according to reason. We could say that these baths, or our own speech, are reasonable, reserving the term "rational" for those who built the baths and for ourselves who are speaking. Reason, then, has its source in a rational soul, and its completion in things done or said reasonably.

32. I can see two things within whose domain reason and the senses can possibly come together: visible human works and audible human words. In either domain, the mind makes use of a necessarily bodily double channel of information: the eyes and the ears. And so, on seeing a whole made up of parts that fit well with one another, it is not absurd to affirm that it appears reasonable. Equally, on hearing a well-composed, harmonious melody, we do not hesitate

rationabiliter sonat. Nemo autem non rideatur, si dixerit: "*Rationabil-iter olet*," aut: "*Rationabiliter sapit*," aut: "*Rationabiliter molle est*," nisi forte in iis quae propter aliquid ab hominibus procurata sunt, ut ita olerent vel saperent vel ferverent, vel quid aliud. Ut si quis locum, unde gravibus odoribus serpentes fugantur, rationabiliter dicat ita olere, causa intuens quare sit factum: aut poculum quod medicus confecerit, rationabiliter amarum esse vel dulce: aut quod temperari languido solium iusserit, calere rationabiliter aut tepere. Nemo autem hortum ingressus et rosam naribus admovens, audet ita dicere: "*Quam rationabiliter fragrat!*" Nec si medicus illam, ut olfaceret, iusserit. Tunc enim praeceptum vel datum illud rationabiliter, non tamen olere rationabiliter dicitur: nec propterea quia naturalis ille odor est. Nam, quamvis a coquo pulmentum condiatur, rationabiliter conditum possumus dicere: rationabiliter autem sapere, cum causa extrinsecus nulla sit, sed praesenti satisfiat voluptati, nullo modo ipsa loquendi consuetudine dicitur.

Si enim quaeratur de illo cui poculum medicus dederit, cur id dulciter sentire debuerit, aliud infertur propter quod ita est, id est morbi genus, quod iam non in illo sensu est sed aliter sese habet in corpore. Si autem rogetur liguriens aliquid, gulae stimulo concitatus, cur ita dulce sit et respondeat, "*Quia libet*," aut: "*quia delector*," nemo illud dicet rationabiliter dulce, nisi forte illius delectatio alicui rei sit necessaria et illud quod mandit ob hoc ita confectum sit.

33. Tenemus, quantum investigare potuimus, quaedam vestigia rationis in sensibus et quod ad visum atque auditum pertinet, in ipsa etiam voluptate. Alii vero sensus non in voluptate sua, sed propter aliquid aliud solent hoc nomen exigere: id autem est rationalis animantis factum propter aliquem finem. Sed ad oculos quod pertinet, in quo congruentia partium rationabilis dicitur, pulchrum appellari solet. Quod vero ad aures, quando rationabilem concentum dicimus cantumque numerosum rationabiliter esse compositum, suavitas vocatur proprio iam nomine. Sed neque in pulchris rebus quod nos color illicit neque in aurium suavitate cum pulsa corda quasi liquide sonat atque pure, rationabile illud

to say that it sounds reasonable. But who would not laugh if we said: it smells, or tastes, reasonable; or: it is reasonably soft, unless he were to apply the remark to man-made things where smell, taste, heat, or whatever had been incorporated in the thing for a purpose. If a place has been treated with a strong-smelling substance in order to keep snakes away, one could say that it smells reasonably, on guessing the cause of it. One could also call a doctor's draught reasonably bitter or reasonably sweet; a bathtub heated on his orders for a weak patient reasonably hot or reasonably lukewarm, both for the same reason. But nobody entering a garden and smelling a rose would dare say: How reasonably it smells! not even if he smelled it on doctor's orders. Although the prescription or the offer itself may be called reasonable, the odor may not, the more so because it is a natural one. When a cook prepares a tasty dish, we can say that it is reasonably seasoned, not that it tastes reasonable. Since nothing external causes its taste but the need to satisfy a present craving, customary language does not allow this kind of usage.

Should we ask one who has been prescribed a potion by the physician why he must have it so sweet, the answer is that he takes it because of the nature of the sickness in the body. The senses have nothing to do with it. But ask the same question to a glutton who drools over whatever excites his senses, and he will answer: "because it is sweet," or: "because I like it." No one would call that taste reasonable, unless dictated by a higher purpose, and the thing that he munches had been concocted for that very purpose.

33. By what we have verified so far, we have detected traces of reason in the senses, especially vision and hearing, but also in pleasure. The other senses can be deemed reasonable not for the pleasure they afford, but for something else: a purpose, which is why a rational animal has been endowed with them. For what pertains to the eyes, a reasonable whole made of parts is said to be beautiful. For the ears, we give the name of sweetness to the reasonable harmony of a choral composition. But we don't call reasonable a striking color to be found in beautiful things, nor do we call reasonable a vibrant sound obtained from plucking a musical string, which produces a clear and pure tone. We are then forced to admit

dicere solemus. Restat ergo ut in istorum sensuum voluptate id ad rationem pertinere fateamur, ubi quaedam dimensio est atque modulatio.

34. Itaque in hoc ipso edificio singula bene considerantes, non possumus non offendi quod unum ostium videmus in latere, alterum prope in medium nec tamen in medio collocatum. Quippe in rebus fabricatis, nulla cogente necessitate, iniqua dimensio partium facere ipsi aspectui velut quamdam videtur iniuriam. Quod autem intus tres fenestrae, una in medio, duae a lateribus, paribus intervallis solio lumen infundunt, quam nos delectat diligentius intuentes quamque in se animum rapit, manifesta res est nec multis verbis vobis aperienda. Unde ipsi architecti iam suo verbo rationem istam vocant et partes discorditer collocatas dicunt non habere rationem.

Quod late patet ac pene in omnes artes operaque humana diffunditur. Iam in carminibus, in quibus item dicimus esse rationem ad voluptatem aurium pertinentem, quis non sentiat dimensionem esse totius huius suavitatis opificem? Sed histrione saltante, cum bene spectantibus gestus illi omnes signa sint rerum, quamvis membrorum numerosus quidam motus oculos eadem illa dimensione delectet, dicitur tamen rationabilis illa saltatio, quod bene aliquid significet et ostendat, excepta sensuum voluptate. Non enim si pennatam Venerem faciat et Cupidinem palliatum, quamvis id mira membrorum motione atque collocatione depingat, oculos videtur offendere, sed per oculos animum, cui rerum signa illa monstrantur: nam oculi offenderentur, si non pulchre moveretur.

Hoc enim pertinebat ad sensum, in quo anima eo ipso quod mixta est corpori percipit voluptatem. Aliud ergo sensus, aliud per sensum: nam sensum mulcet pulcher motus, per sensum autem animum solum pulchra in motu significatio. Hoc etiam in auribus facilius advertitur, nam quidquid iucunde sonat, illud ipsum auditum libet atque illicit, quod autem per eumdem sonum bene significatur, nuntio quidem aurium sed ad solam mentem refertur. Itaque cum audimus illos versus:

Quid tantum oceano properent se tingere soles
Hiberni, vel quae tardis mora noctibus obstet?

that it is reason that delights in the pleasure of the senses, through dimension in the case of the eyes and through modulation in the case of the ears.

34. On paying attention to detail within the same building, we cannot but find it amiss to see one opening on a side, and another in the middle but not quite. To construct something without there being a need for it, without regard to proportion, looks as if a deliberate injury is inflicted to its appearance. There is no need to use many words to tell you how three windows, one in the middle and two at the sides, opened at equal intervals, have the effect of lighting the bath, delighting our senses and inducing contemplation to our soul. That is why architects give the name "design" to such an arrangement, and decry the lack of it ("design" is another word for purpose) to be found in the disordered arrangement of architectural elements.

This is obvious everywhere, and the same understanding obtains in all forms of human endeavor. Take song and verse, for instance. We have already seen that it is reason that delights in the pleasure of the ear. Who fails to perceive that dimension and rhythm are the basis for that sweetness? But in the case of a dancing actor, the rhythmic motions of his members are to the eager spectators signs of realities beyond the pleasure of the senses. Although their eyes may delight at the harmony and succession of movements, they may deem such a dance as reasonable. Were he to represent a winged Venus and a cloaked Cupid by means of skillful motion and placing of hands and feet, the spectators' eyes would not be offended, but their souls would, on interpreting the idea conveyed by those movements. The eyes would indeed be offended if the motions were clumsy.

It is the senses that perceive motion, but since the soul is united to the body, it is the soul that delights in it. The senses in themselves are therefore one reality, and entirely another as means to convey information to the soul. A lovely movement charms the senses, but only the beautiful meaning behind that movement charms the soul. It is easier to understand this with the sense of hearing: a beautiful sound pleases the ear by entering it, but whatever that sound means only the mind can grasp. On hearing the verse:

> *Why the winter sun lingers so much to enter the ocean,*
> *and what shackles the long, interminable nights?*

aliter metra laudamus, aliterque sententiam: nec sub eodem intellectu dicimus "*rationabiliter sonat*" et "*rationabiliter dictum est*" [Virgil, *Georgica* 2, 480–81]

CAPUT XII

Disciplinarum omnium excogitatrix ratio. Occasio vocabulorum, litterarum et numerorum. Occasio discretionis syllabarum et verborum. Occasio historiae.

35. Ergo iam tria genera sunt rerum in quibus illud rationabile apparet. Unum est in factis ad aliquem finem relatis, alterum in dicendo, tertium in delectando. Primum nos admonet nihil temere facere, secundum, recte docere, ultimum, beate contemplari. In moribus est illud superius, haec autem duo in disciplinis de quibus nunc agimus. Namque illud quod in nobis est rationale, id est quod ratione utitur et rationabilia vel facit vel sequitur, quia naturali quodam vinculo in eorum societate astringebatur, cum quibus illi erat ratio ipsa communis, nec homini homo firmissime sociari posset nisi colloquerentur atque ita sibi mentes suas cogitationesque quasi refunderent, vidit esse imponenda rebus vocabula, id est significantes quosdam sonos, ut, quoniam sentire animos suos non poterant, ad eos sibi copulandos sensu quasi interprete uterentur. Sed audiri absentium verba non poterant; ergo illa ratio peperit litteras, notatis omnibus oris ac linguae sonis atque discretis. Nihil autem horum facere poterat, si multitudo rerum sine quodam defixo termino infinite patere videretur. Ergo utilitas numerandi magna necessitate animadversa est. Quibus duobus repertis, nata est illa librariorum et calculonum professio, velut quaedam grammaticae infantia, quam Varro *litterationem* vocat: graece quomodo appelletur, non satis in praesentia recolo.

36. Progressa deinde ratio animadvertit eosdem oris sonos quibus loqueremur et quos litteris iam signaverat, alios esse qui moderato varie hiatu, quasi enodati ac simplices faucibus sine ulla collisione defluerent, alios diverso pressu oris, tenere tamen

we praise the meter by one standard, and the sentence by another. By the first, "it sounds reasonable;" by the second, "it makes sense."

TWELVE
Reason devised all the disciplines. The birth of words, writing and numbers. The separation of words into syllables. The birth of history.

35. We have surveyed three types of things where the work of reason makes its appearance. The first is things constructed for a purpose, the second for speech, and the last for pleasure. The first is about not acting rashly; the second, about teaching the truth; the last, about contemplation. The first applies to right living, the second and third to the disciplines we are now analyzing. Our rational power, i.e. our using reason in doing or understanding reasonable things, saw the necessity of giving things names. This was necessary because reason, common to all in a human society, forms the most natural bond between humans. But no firm bonding can take place at all without *communication*, by which thoughts are mutually exchanged. Now *words* are no more than sounds with meaning. They make use of the senses as conveyors of thought, since the latter cannot be directly transmitted from one person to another. Even so, the senses could not hear the words of the absent, and so reason begat *writing*, sorting out all the sounds and pauses of mouth and tongue. None of these would have been possible, however, if things, as limitless as they appear, had not been given some kind of fixed domain. And so the need for *numbers* was seen as paramount. With the invention of these two, there were also born the professions of copyist and calculator. Varro calls this infancy of grammar *literacy*, the Greek name of which escapes me now.

36. Going further, reason discovered a difference in the *sounds* we utter in speaking and signify in writing. Some flow clear and simple out of the mouth on moderately opening it; others need different degrees of compression of the lips, others yet are not produced

aliquem sonum; extremos autem qui nisi adiunctis sibi primis erumpere non valerent. Itaque litteras hoc ordine quo expositae sunt *vocales, semivocales* et *mutas* nominavit. Deinde syllabas notavit, deinde verba in octo genera formasque digesta sunt omnisque illorum motus, integritas, iunctura, perite subtiliterque distincta sunt. Inde iam numerorum et dimensionis non immemor, adiecit animum in ipsa vocum et syllabarum varias moras atque inde spatia temporis alia dupla, alia simpla esse comperit, quibus longe brevesque syllabae tenderentur. Notavit etiam ista et in regulas certas disposuit.

37. Poterat iam perfecta esse grammatica, sed quia ipso nomine profiteri se litteras clamat, unde etiam latine *litteratura* dicitur, factum est ut quidquid dignum memoria litteris mandaretur ad eam necessario pertineret. Itaque unum quidem nomen, sed res infinita, multiplex, curarum plenior quam iucunditatis aut veritatis, huic disciplinae accessit historia, non tam ipsis historicis quam grammaticis laboriosa. Quis enim ferat imperitum videri hominem qui volasse Daedalum non audierit, mendacem illum qui finxerit, stultum qui crediderit, impudentem qui interrogaverit non videri? Aut in quo nostros familiares graviter miserari soleo, qui si non responderint quid vocata sit mater Euryali, accusantur inscitiae, cum ipsi eos, a quibus ea rogantur, vanos et ineptos et curiosos audeant appellare?

CAPUT XIII
Dialectices et rhetorices inventio

38. Illa igitur ratio perfecta dispositaque grammatica, admonita est quaerere atque attendere hanc ipsam vim qua peperit artem: nam eam definiendo, distribuendo, colligendo, non solum digesserat atque ordinaverat, verum ab omni etiam falsitatis irreptione defenderat. Quando ergo transiret ad alia fabricanda, nisi ipsa sua prius quasi quaedam machinamenta et instrumenta distingueret, notaret, digereret proderetque ipsam disciplina disciplinarum, quam *dialecticam* vocant? Haec docet docere, haec

unless the lips are closed first and then suddenly opened. It called the first type of sounds *vowels*, the second *fricatives*, and the last *plosives*. Next, it formalized the *syllables*, and then classified words into eight *parts of speech* according to *form*. Their *morphology*, *usage*, and *syntax* were most skillfully and subtly worked out. Then, lest it leave out rhythm and quantity, reason paid special attention to various types of voice, stops, or pauses, according to which it discovered that syllables could be arranged into long and short, depending on the time intervals they needed. It added this information and established certain rules for everything.

37. *Grammar* could now be considered complete. But as its name says, grammar is for writing, which is what literature means in Latin. As a result, whatever is worth committing to memory in writing is also part and parcel of grammar. And that is how *history* got into the picture, for under that name there lies an array of facts causing more worries than truth and delight, and making it equally burdensome to historians and grammarians. Who would deem as genuinely ignorant someone who never heard of Daedalus's flight, or called the inventor of the story a liar, and the one who believed it a fool and him who asked questions about it shameless? Or take what makes me feel sorry for those friends of ours who, on failing to answer who Euryalus's mother was, dared call the questioners vain, inept, and curious!

THIRTEEN
Invention of logic and rhetoric

38. As reason brought grammar to perfection, it sought to take care of itself, the very power by which it produced that art. It not only analyzed and ordered itself, but further defended itself against the infiltration of falsehood. How could it then pass on to other matters, without first distinguishing, bringing out and ordering the tools of its own trade, and so creating that discipline of all disciplines known as *logic*? This discipline teaches how to teach, and how to learn. In it, reason shows itself for what it is,

docet discere; in hac se ipsa ratio demonstrat atque aperit quae sit, quid velit, quid valeat. Scit scire; sola scientes facere non solum vult, sed etiam potest.

Verum quoniam plerumque stulti homines ad ea quae suadentur recte, utiliter et honeste, non ipsam sincerissimam quam rarus animus videt veritatem, sed proprios sensus consuetudinemque sectantur, oportebat eos non doceri solum quantum queunt, sed saepe et maxime commoveri. Hanc suam partem quae id ageret, necessitatis pleniorem quam puritatis, refertissimo gremio deliciarum, quas populo spargat ut ad utilitatem suam dignetur adduci, vocavit *rhetoricam.* Hactenus pars illa quae in significando rationabilis dicitur, studiis liberalibus disciplinisque promota est.

CAPUT XIV
Musica et poetica. Versus.

39. Hinc se illa ratio ad ipsarum divinarum beatissimam contemplationem rapere voluit. Sed ne de alto caderet, quaesivit gradus atque ipsa sibi viam per suas possessiones ordinemque molita est. Desiderabat enim pulchritudinem, quam sola et simplex posset sine istis oculis intueri; impediebatur a sensibus. Itaque in eos ipsos paululum aciem torsit, qui veritatem sese habere clamantes, festinantem ad alia pergere importuno strepitu revocabant. Et primo ab auribus coepit, quia dicebant ipsa verba sua esse, quibus iam et grammaticam et dialecticam et rhetoricam fecerat. At ista potentissima secernendi cito vidit quid inter sonum et id cuius signum esset distaret. Intellexit nihil aliud ad aurium iudicium pertinere, quam sonum eumque esse triplicem: aut in voce animantis, aut in eo quod flatus in organis faceret, aut in eo quod pulsu ederetur. Ad primum pertinere tragoedos vel comoedos, vel choros cuiuscemodi atque omnes omnino qui voce propria canerent: secundum tibiis et similibus instrumentis deputari: tertio dari citharas, lyras, cymbala, atque omne quod percutiendo canorum esset.

40. Videbat autem hanc materiam esse vilissimam, nisi certa dimensione temporum et acuminis gravitatisque moderata varietate

what it wants, what it can do. It knows that it knows. It alone is both willing and capable of making people learned.

In truth, however, most people are fools, so that they are led to what is right, useful, and good by their senses rather than by unadulterated truth, which very few selected souls see. It was therefore necessary that such people should be taught not so much with regard to their capacity, but often and above all by arousing their passions. Reason called this art *rhetoric*, assigning to it the necessary but by no means simple task of scattering charms and delight among the crowd, with the intent of turning it towards what is good for it. That is how high the liberal arts have succeeded in raising reason.

FOURTEEN
Music and poetry. Verse.

39. From here, reason wanted to take off into the heights of contemplation of divine things. Not to fall off those heights, though, it sought to climb in steps along a path hewn by its own devices. It sought that beauty which can exclusively be attained in simplicity without bodily eyes, but the senses stood in the way. Therefore it slowly turned its attention towards those same senses. These, staking a claim for the possession of truth, distracted it from its pursuit of higher things with their oppressive clatter. The ears were first, claiming as their possession the very words which had served as the basis for grammar, logic, and rhetoric. By its immense powers of analysis, however, reason saw at once the difference between a sound and the reality it symbolized. It understood that the only thing the ears can do is to sort out sounds into three kinds: the human voice, wind, and percussion instruments. Tragedians, comedians, choirs, and all those who in one way or another sing, produce the first. Trumpets and similar things, the second. Guitars, harps, drums, and anything else that on being hit produces a sound, the third.

40. Reason also noticed that all of this was worth very little without regular timing and a variety of high and low pitch sounds.

soni figurarentur. Recognovit hinc esse illa semina quae in grammatica, cum syllabas diligenti consideratione versaret, pedes et accentus vocaverat. Et quia in ipsis verbis brevitates et longitudines syllabarum prope aequali multitudine sparsas in oratione attendere facile fuit, tentavit pedes illos in ordines certos disponere atque coniungere et in eo primo sensum ipsum secuta, moderatos impressit articulos, quae et *caesa* et *membra* nominavit. Et ne longius pedum cursus provolveretur quam eius iudicium possit sustinere, modum statuit unde reverteretur et ab eo ipso *versum* vocavit. Quod autem non esset certo fine moderatum, sed tamen rationabiliter ordinatis pedibus curreret, *rhythmi* nomine notavit, qui latine nihil aliud quam *numerus* dici potuit. Sic ab ea poetae geniti sunt: in quibus cum videret non solum sonorum, sed etiam verborum rerumque magna momenta, plurimum eos honoravit eisque tribuit quorum vellent rationabilium mendaciorum potestatem. Et quoniam de prima illa disciplina stirpem ducebant, iudices in eos grammaticos esse permisit.

41. In hoc igitur quarto gradu, sive in rhythmis, sive in ipsa modulatione intellegebat regnare numeros totumque perficere: inspexit diligentissime cuiusmodi essent; reperiebat divinos et sempiternos, praesertim quod ipsis auxiliantibus omnia superiora contexuerat. Et iam tolerabat aegerrime splendorem illorum atque serenitatem corporea vocum materia decolorari. Et quoniam illud quod mens videt semper est praesens et immortale approbatur, cuius generis numeri apparebant, sonus autem quia sensibilis res est praeterfluit in praeteritum tempus imprimiturque memoriae, rationabili mendacio iam poetis favente ratione (quaerendumne quid propagini similiter inesset?), Iovis et Memoriae filias Musas esse confictum est. Unde ista disciplina sensus intellectusque particeps *musicae* nomen invenit.

CAPUT XV
Geometria et astronomia

42. Hinc est profecta in oculorum opes et terram caelumque collustrans, sensit nihil aliud quam pulchritudinem sibi placere, et in

Reason found an application here of what it had called meter and stress in grammar, when it diligently analyzed syllables. Since it had been easy to identify long and short syllables evenly distributed in prose sentences, it attempted to distribute and combine meter in the same fashion. Following the same sense of hearing in the first, it divided the sentences into certain measures, calling them stops and clauses as the case may be. And to prevent the sequence of meter from going on and on beyond reason, it established boundaries with room for some repetition, hence the name "verse". What was not encompassed by a fixed boundary, but still run in a certain order of meter, it called rhythm, which is the same as number. This is how reason begat *poetry*; and seeing in poets' work the combined strength of words and rhyme, gave them a special place of honor, together with the license to compose any fiction they wished, but within reason. And since poets drew their matter primarily from grammar, the first of the disciplines in time, reason gave grammarians the power to judge poets.

41. At this fourth level, reason understood that number, both in rhythm and modulation, was supreme and all-encompassing. It scrutinized number, therefore, most minutely. When reason realized that with the help of number it had organized all the foregoing, it called number divine and almost eternal. And so it grievously tolerated that the splendor and purity of number should be somewhat clouded by the material sound of voices. Now number is a mental construct and, as such, ever present in the mind and understood as immortal. Sound, on the other hand, is temporary and fleeting, but can be memorized. As a result poets, with the leave of reason, created the fiction that Jupiter fathered the Muses from Mnemosyne (Memory). Good luck to their progeny, if any, but this hybrid of senses and mind came to be called *music*.

plural Lt.

FIFTEEN
Geometry and astronomy

42. From here, reason stepped onto the domain of the eyes. Surveying the earth and the heavens, it found that nothing but

pulchritudine figuras, et in figuris dimensiones, in dimensionibus numeros; quaesivitque ipsa secum utrum ibi talis linea talisque rotunditas vel quaelibet alia forma et figura esset, qualem intellegentia contineret. Longe deteriorem invenit et nulla ex parte quod viderent oculi cum eo quod mens cerneret comparandum. Haec quoque distincta et disposita in disciplinam redegit appellavitque *geometriam*. Motus eam caeli multum movebat et ad se diligenter considerandum invitabat. Etiam ibi per constantissimas temporum vices, per astrorum ratos definitosque cursus, per intervallorum spatia moderata, intellexit nihil aliud quam illam dimensionem numerosque dominari. Quae similiter definiendo ac secernendo in ordinem nectens, *astrologiam* genuit, magnum religiosis argumentum tormentumque curiosis.

43. In his igitur omnibus disciplinis occurrebant ei omnia numerosa, quae tamen in illis dimensionibus manifestius eminebant, quas in seipsa cogitando atque volvendo intuebatur verissimas: in his autem quae sentiuntur, umbras earum potius atque vestigia recolebat. Hic se multum erexit multumque praesumpsit; ausa est immortalem animam comprobare. Tractavit omnia diligenter, percepit prorsus se plurimum posse et quidquid posset, numeris posse. Movit eam quoddam miraculum et suspicari coepit seipsam fortasse numerum esse eum ipsum quo cuncta numerarentur, aut si id non esset, ibi tamen eum esse quo pervenire satageret. Hunc vero totis viribus comprehendit, qui iam universae veritatis index futurus, ille cuius mentionem fecit Alypius, cum de Academicis quaereremus quasi Proteus in manibus erat. Imagines enim falsae rerum earum quas numeramus, ab illo occultissimo quo numeramus defluentes, in sese rapiunt cogitationem et saepe illum cum iam tenetur elabi faciunt.

CAPUT XVI
Disciplinae liberales intellectum efferunt ad divina

44. Quibus si quisque non cesserit et illa omnia quae per tot disciplinas late varieque diffusa sunt, ad unum quoddam simplex

beauty pleased it: within beauty forms, within forms proportion, within proportion number. It asked itself where in the real world this or that straight, curved, or other line as conceived by the intelligence might be. It found reality far inferior. Nothing real stood comparison with what the mind could see. It analyzed these forms one by one and arranged them into a discipline which it called *geometry*. The motion of the heavens next gripped its attention, inviting reason to scrutinize it. There it also understood that the recurring seasons, the fixed determined pathways of the heavenly bodies, and the intervals of space between them responded to numerical proportion. Defining and sorting out all these, connected them in the order called *astrology*, an ever-impressing argument for the religiously minded and mental torture for the merely curious.

43. All that came to the attention of reason in all these branches of learning did so in harmony. This was especially manifest in the ideal proportions born of reason and reflected upon therein. It found them most true, but what could be detected by the senses was only a shadow or faint footmark of that reflection. Here reason became proud and presumptuous: it dared prove that the soul is immortal. It investigated everything most diligently, finding that it had great power, and that such power was none other than number power. A wonderful suspicion now began to prod it, that itself might be that very number principle of all things. If not, number was the end and aim of its journey. It clung on to it with all its strength, considering number as the future holder of all truth. Alypius, in our quarrel with the Academicians, deemed it as a kind of Proteus in their hands. The false images of things countable, however, distract us from that most hidden principle and attract our mind to themselves, often obliterating previous knowledge from it.

SIXTEEN
The liberal arts lead the mind to God

44. The truly learned are those who, not allowing all the different realities to distract them, attempt their unification into a simple,

verum certumque redegerit, eruditi nomine dignissimus, non temere iam quaerit illa divina, non iam credenda solum, verum etiam contemplanda, intellegenda atque retinenda. Quisquis autem vel adhuc servus cupiditatum, et inhians rebus pereuntibus, vel iam ista fugiens casteque vivens, nesciens tamen quid sit nihil, quid informis materia, quid formatum exanime, quid corpus, quid species in corpore, quid locus, quid tempus, quid in loco, quid in tempore, quid motus secundum locum, quid motus non secundum locum, quid stabilis motus, quid sit aevum, quid sit nec in loco esse, nec nusquam, et quid sit praeter tempus et semper, quid sit et nusquam esse et nusquam non esse, et numquam esse et numquam non esse: quisquis ergo ista nesciens, non dico de summo illo Deo, qui scitur melius nesciendo, sed de anima ipsa sua quaerere ac disputare voluerit, tantum errabit quantum errari plurimum potest: facilius autem cognoscet ista, qui numeros simplices atque intellegibiles comprehenderit. Porro istos comprehendet, qui et ingenio valens et privilegio aetatis aut cuiuslibet felicitatis otiosus et studio vehementer incensus, memoratum disciplinarum ordinem, quantum satis est, fuerit persecutus. Cum enim artes illae omnes liberales, partim ad usum vitae, partim ad cognitionem rerum contemplationemque discantur, usum earum assequi difficillimum est nisi ei qui ab ipsa pueritia ingeniosissimus instantissime atque constantissime operam dederit.

CAPUT XVII
Arduas questiones ne attingant non instructi disciplinis

45. Quod vero ex illis ad id quod quaerimus opus est, ne te, quaeso, mater, haec velut rerum immensa quaedam silva deterreat. Etenim quaedam de omnibus eligentur numero paucissima, vi potentissima, cognitione autem multis quidem ardua; tibi tamen, cuius ingenium quotidie mihi novum est et cuius animum vel aetate vel admirabili temperantia remotissimum ab omnibus nugis et a magna labe corporis emergentem, in se multum surrexisse cognosco, tam erunt facilia quam difficilia tardissimis miserrimeque viventibus. Si enim dicam te facile ad eum sermonem perventuram, qui locutionis et linguae vitio careat, perfecto mentiar.

true, and certain whole. Having done so, they can soar on to divine realities not rashly and by faith alone, but contemplating, understanding, and retaining them. These realities are forbidden to the slaves of pleasure, or to those hankering after perishing things. But even those who flee from such and live a clean life can be ignorant of nothingness, of formless matter, of the form of inanimate things, of body, of species, of space and time, of being in space and in time, of local motion, of change in general, of uniform motion, of eternity, of what it is to be nowhere, or to be beyond time, or to be and not to be somewhere. He who is ignorant of all that, and so much as wishes to investigate and argue about his own soul, let alone about the Most High, who is better known by remaining ignorant, will fall into all possible types of error. It is much easier to come to such knowledge by understanding the simple and rational numbers. To go further, one has to have a good mind, be of mature age, enjoy leisure, and have enthusiasm for study, enough to pursue the order of the disciplines just analyzed. Getting acquainted with the liberal arts, however, whether pursued for the sake of usefulness or for the sake of knowledge and contemplation, is extremely difficult. It is necessary to be most clever and to start from childhood with unfaltering attention and perseverance.

SEVENTEEN

The uninstructed should not tackle matters above their heads

45. You, mother, please don't be put off by this seemingly huge forest of things needed to get on with our inquiry. Very few such things will be chosen out of the lot, but most powerful ones, which are certainly difficult for most to grasp. Not for you, though: I learn new things from your great mind every day. I know your high character, free from all material trifles and rising above bodily corruption. You have attained it either because of age or because of your marvelous temperance. These matters will be as easy for you as they are difficult for the dull, who live a life of misery. Were I to say that you would easily attain a speech free from

Me enim ipsum, cui magna necessitas fuit ista perdiscere, adhuc in multis verborum sonis Itali exagitant et a me vicissim, quod ad ipsum sonum attinet, reprehenduntur. Aliud est enim esse arte, aliud gente securum. Soloecismos autem quos dicimus , fortasse quisque doctus diligenter attendens in oratione mea reperiet; non enim defuit qui mihi nonnulla huiusmodi vitia ipsum Ciceronem fecisse peritissime persuaserit. Barbarismorum autem genus nostris temporibus tale compertum est ut et ipsa eius oratio barbara videatur, qua Roma servata est. Sed tu, contemptis istis vel puerilibus rebus, vel ad te non pertinentibus, ita grammaticae pene divinam vim naturamque cognoscis, ut eius animam tenuisse, corpus reliquisse disertis videaris.

46. Hoc etiam de ceteris huiusmodi artibus dixerim: quas si penitus fortasse contemnis, admoneo te, quantum filius audeo quantumque permittis, ut fidem istam tuam, quam venerandis mysteriis percepisti, firme cauteque custodias, deinde ut in hac vita atque moribus constanter vigilanterque permaneas.

De rebus autem obscurissimis et tamen divinis, quomodo Deus et nihil mali faciat et sit omnipotens, et tanta mala fiant, et cui bono mundum fecerit, qui non erat indigus, et utrum semper fuerit malum an tempore coeperit, et, si semper fuit, utrum sub conditione Dei fuerit: et, si fuit, utrum etiam iste mundus semper fuerit, in quo illud malum divino ordine dominaretur; si autem hic mundus aliquando esse coepit, quomodo antequam esset, potestate Dei malum tenebatur, et quid opus erat mundum fabricari, quo malum quod iam Dei potestas frenabat, ad poenas animarum includeretur, si autem fuit tempus quo sub Dei dominio malum non erat, quid subito accidit, quod per aeterna retro tempora non acciderat. In Deo enim novum exstitisse consilium, ne dicam impium, ineptissimum est dicere. Si autem importunum fuisse et quasi improbum malum Deo dicimus, quod nonnulli existimant, iam nemo doctus risum tenebit, nemo non succensebit indoctus. Quid enim potuit Deo nocere mali nescio qua illa natura? Si enim dicunt non potuisse, fabricandi mundi causa non erit: si potuisse dicunt, inexpiabile nefas est Deum violabilem credere, nec ita saltem, ut vel virtute providerit, ne sua substantia violaretur. Namque animam

errors of grammar and pronunciation, I would lie through my teeth. I had to learn these things out of professional need, yet the Italians still correct my pronunciation of many words, and I in turn correct theirs. It is one thing to be certain in theory, another in practice with people. It is perfectly possible that an expert, upon examination, should find blunders in my speech. There was indeed one who argued with me most convincingly that the great Cicero himself had made quite a few such blunders. So many alien words have been recently introduced in the language that even his famous speech by which he saved Rome would seem foreign today. You, however, holding all this stuff beneath contempt, know the divine power and nature of grammar so well, as to possess the grain, as it were, leaving the chaff to the experts.

46. I would go on, saying the same thing of all the other arts. You may despise them all, perhaps: except, let me warn you as a daring son and with your leave, for this faith which you practice through the sacred mysteries. Keep it firmly and cautiously, so as to remain faithful and vigilant in this life.

There remains an array of most obscure matters concerning God: How can He be almighty without doing evil, why is there so much evil, for whom did He make a world that He did not need? Did evil always exist, or did it have its beginning in time? If it always was, was it submitted to God, and if so, was also this world full of evil under God's control? If this world also had a beginning, how did God's power hold evil in check before creation? What should the world be made for, if this evil that existed before had to be included in it for the ruin of souls? If there was a time when God did not hold sway over evil, what suddenly happened which had not happened before? It is most inept, if not impious, to affirm that God may have had second thoughts. If we agree with those who say that evil was unsuitable, and even bad, for God, the learned will laugh and the unlearned will feel indignant. What "nature" of evil could have harmed God? If evil could not harm Him, the creation of the world would have had no reason to be; if it could do harm, it would be the maximum of impiety to say that God is liable to harm of any kind without granting Him the power to prevent harm to Himself. They say so because

poenas hic pendere fatentur, cum inter eius et Dei substantiam nihil velint omnino distare. Si autem istum mundum non factum dicamus, impium est atque ingratum credere, ne illud sequatur quod Deus eum non fabricarit: ergo de his atque huiusmodi rebus, aut ordine illo eruditionis, aut nullo modo quidquam requirendum est.

CAPUT XVIII
Quo ordine provehitur anima ad cognitionem sui et ipsius unitatis

47. Et ne quisquam latissimum aliquid nos complexos esse arbitretur, hoc dico planius atque brevius. Ad istarum rerum cognitionem neminem aspirare debere sine illa quasi duplici scientia bonae disputationis potentiaeque numerorum. Si quis etiam hoc plurimum putat, solos numeros optime noverit aut solam dialecticam. Si et hoc infinitum est, tantum perfecte sciat quid sit unum in numeris quantumque valeat nondum in illa summa lege summoque ordine rerum omnium, sed in iis quae quotidie passim sentimus atque agimus. Excipit enim hanc eruditionem iam ipsa philosophiae disciplina, et in ea nihil plus invenit quam quid sit unum, sed longe altius longeque divinius. Cuius duplex quaestio est: una de anima, altera de Deo. Prima efficit ut nosmetipsos noverimus; altera, ut originem nostram. Illa nobis dulcior, ista carior, illa nos dignos beata vita, beatos haec facit; prima est illa discentibus, ista iam doctis. Hic est ordo studiorum sapientiae, per quem fit quisque idoneus ad intelligendum ordinem rerum, id est ad dignoscendos duos mundos et ipsum parentem universitatis, cuius nulla scientia est in anima, nisi scire quomodo eum nesciat.

48. Hunc igitur ordinem tenens anima iam philosophiae tradita, primo seipsam inspicit; et cui iam illa eruditio persuasit, aut suam aut seipsam esse rationem, in ratione autem aut nihil esse melius et potentius numeris, aut nihil aliud quam numerum esse rationem, ita secum loquetur: Ego quodam meo motu interiore et occulto, et quae discenda sunt possum discernere et connectere, et haec vis mea ratio vocatur. Quid autem discernendum est, nisi quod aut unum putatur et non est, aut certe non tam unum est quam putatur? Item, cur quid connectendum est, nisi ut unum fiat

they believe that there is no difference between God's substance and that of suffering souls. If we say that this world was not made, it would be a show of impiety and ingratitude, for it would follow that God has not created it. Clearly in all such matters one either follows the correct order of learning, or leaves them altogether.

EIGHTEEN
What order leads the soul to the knowledge of self and of unity

47. Lest anyone think that I have bitten off more than I can chew, I will explain and summarize. No one should attempt to know such things without the two sciences of logic and mathematics. Should both prove too much, let one stick either to one or to the other. But even if this seems excessive, let him appreciate unity and its power in number, not so much in the supreme law of order that governs all things, as in those things we see and do here and there every day. Philosophy also hankers after unity, but in a much higher and more divine way. It follows two lines of inquiry: the soul and God. Through the first we know ourselves, what we are; through the second, our origin, where we come from. The former is more pleasant; the latter more valuable. The first makes us worthy of happiness; the second makes us actually happy. They are for the learners and the learned respectively. This is the order or wisdom of the curriculum. By following it, one becomes fit to understand the order of things: two worlds and God their common origin. But the soul knows nothing of God, except that it is ignorant and why.

48. Holding on to the previous order, the soul given to philosophy looks at itself first. Convinced by that learning that it possesses reason to the extent of identifying with it, and that number is reason's most powerful weapon, it will so reflect: "An interior and hidden power has enabled me to distinguish among the subjects of learning and to connect them as necessary. This power is called reason. But what is to be distinguished except what appears to be one and is not, or what it is certainly not as one as believed? Equally, what is to be connected except what needs to be made

quantum potest? Ergo et in discernendo et in connectendo unum volo, et unum amo. Sed cum discerno, purgatum, cum connecto, integrum volo. In illa parte vitantur aliena, in hac propria copulantur, ut unum aliquid perfectum fiat.

Lapis ut esset lapis, omnes eius partes omnisque natura in unum solidata est. Quid arbor? Nonne arbor non esset, si una non esset? Quid membra cuiuslibet animantis ac viscera et quidquid est eorum e quibus constat? Certe si unitatis patiantur divortium, non erit animal. Amici quid aliud quam unum esse conantur? Et quanto magis unum, tanto magis amici sunt. Populus una civitas est, cui est periculosa dissensio: quid est autem dissentire, nisi non unum sentire? Ex multis militibus fit unus exercitus: nonne quaevis multitudo eo minus vincitur, quo magis in unum coit? Unde ipsa coitio in unum *cuneus* nominatus est, quasi co-uneus. Quid amor omnis? Nonne unum vult fieri cum eo quod amat, et si ei contingat, unum cum eo fit? Voluptas ipsa non ob aliud delectat vehementius, nisi quod amantia sese corpora in unum coguntur. Dolor unde perniciosus est? Quia id quod unum erat dissicere nititur. Ergo molestum et periculosum est cum eo unum fieri quod separari potest.

CAPUT XIX
Homo unde brutis praestantior. Quomodo possit videre Deum.

49. Ex multis rebus passim ante iacentibus, deinde in unam formam congregatis, unam facio domum. Melior ego, siquidem ego facio, illa fit: ideo melior quia facio, non dubium est inde me esse meliorem quam domus est. Sed non inde sum melior hirundine aut apicula, nam et illa nidos affabre struit et illa favos: sed his melior, quia rationale animal sum. At si in ratis dimensionibus ratio est, numquidnam et aves quod fabricant minus apte congruenterque dimensum est? Imo numerosissimum est. Non ergo numerosa faciendo, sed numeros cognoscendo melior sum. Quid ergo? Illae nescientes operari numerosa poterant? Poterant, profecto. Unde id docetur? Ex eo quod nos quoque certis dimensionibus linguam dentibus et palato accommodamus, ut ex ore litterae ac verba prorumpant, nec tamen cogitamus cum loquimur quo motu oris id

one insofar as possible? Therefore in both operations unity is what I want and love. In analysis, I seek unity purified; in synthesis I seek it whole." The former excludes what does not belong; the latter unites all things that belong together. Perfect unity is the result.

For a stone to be such, all its parts need to coalesce into unity. What is a tree? Would it be a tree without unity? And what about the members, viscera, and all the parts an animal consists of? Once dismembered, an animal ceases to be such. Do not friends seek unity in friendship? The more they attain it, the friendlier they become. A people is a unity of citizens, for whom nothing is more dangerous than dissension. What does "to dissent" mean if not "to think differently"? An army consists of many fighting men. Is it not true that such a number is the more undefeatable, the more united it is? Such a union truly becomes like a wedge or *coin*, from *co-union*. Isn't it the same with love of all kinds? Does it not want to become one in consummation with the loved one? Pleasure itself is so intense, because the lovers achieve bodily union. Why, on the other hand, is sorrow painful? Because it attempts to undo unity. To force unity on what can be separated is therefore to invite trouble and danger.

NINETEEN
Excellence of man over the animals. How he can see God.

49. I build a house by assembling into one single design a variety of materials previously scattered here and there. I am superior to the house because I am the one that builds it. The house is the one that gets built. There is no doubt that I am superior to the house precisely because of my building it. In this sense I am not better than a swallow or a bee, which builds nest and honeycomb so skillfully. I am better for being a rational animal. But if correct proportions are the fruit of reason, are nest-building birds using anything less than correct proportions? Not at all. Their proportions are perfect. But I am still superior not for making things according to measure, but for knowing what measure is. What then? Can they do things without knowing what they are doing? Certainly. How do we know? From our adapting tongue to palate

facere debeamus. Deinde quis bonus cantator, etiam si musicae sit imperitus, non ipso sensu naturali et rhythmum et melos perceptum memoria custodiat in canendo? Quo quid fieri numerosius potest? Hoc nescit indoctus, sed tamen facit operante natura. Quando autem melior et pecoribus praeponendus? Quando novit quod facit. At nihil aliud me pecori praeponit, nisi quod rationale animal sum.

50. Quomodo igitur immortalis est ratio et ego simul et rationale et mortale quiddam esse definior? An ratio non est immortalis? Sed unum ad duo vel duo ad quatuor verissima ratio est: nec magis heri fuit ista ratio vera quam hodie, nec magis cras aut post annum erit vera, nec si omnis iste mundus concidat, poterit ista ratio non esse. Ista enim semper talis est, mundus autem iste nec heri habuit, nec cras habebit quod habet hodie, nec hodierno ipso die vel spatio unius horae eodem loco solem habuit: ita cum in eo nihil manet, nihil vero parvo spatio temporis habet eodem modo. Igitur si immortalis est ratio et ego qui ista omnia vel discerno vel connecto ratio sum, illud quo mortale appellor non est meum. Aut si anima non id est quod ratio et tamen ratione utor et per rationem melior sum, a deteriore ad melius, a mortali ad immortale fugiendum est.

Haec et alia multa secum anima bene erudita loquitur atque agitat: quae persequi nolo, ne, cum ordinem vos docere cupio, modum excedam qui pater est ordinis. Gradatim enim se et ad mores vitamque optimam non iam sola fide, sed certa ratione perducit. Cui numerorum vim atque potentiam diligenter intuenti nimis indignum videbitur et nimis flendum, per suam scientiam versum bene currere citharamque concinere et suam vitam seque ipsam quae anima est devium iter sequi et dominante sibi libidine cum turpissimo se vitiorum strepitu dissonare.

51. Cum autem se composuerit et ordinaverit ac concinnam pulchramque reddiderit, audebit iam Deum videre, atque ipsum fontem unde manat omne verum ipsumque Patrem Veritatis. Deus magne, qui erunt illi oculi! Quam sani, quam decori, quam valentes, quam constantes, quam sereni, quam beati! Quid autem

and teeth so as to produce words. We don't think beforehand how we should move the mouth while speaking. Doesn't a good singer, even though ignorant of music, reproduce the melody and rhythm from memory and musical sense? What is more proportionate than this? The ignorant man does not know this, but still acts according to nature. Why then should man be deemed superior to cattle? Because he knows what he does. Nothing more than rationality keeps me above the brutes.

50. How is reason immortal then, and I am defined as something both rational and mortal? Is reason not immortal after all? One to two equals two to four is a truest ratio (another name for reason). It was not truer yesterday than it is today, nor will it be truer tomorrow, or in a year's time. It would not cease to be true even if the world came to an end. It is always the same, while this world did not have yesterday, nor will it have tomorrow, what it has today. The sun changes place continuously within one hour. As nothing is permanent, everything is subjected to change within a very short time. If reason is then immortal, and I, who distinguish and connect, am reason, what causes my being, which is called mortal, is not mine. But if the soul is none other than reason, which I use and which makes me a superior being, this binds me to become ever better, up to immortality itself.

The learned soul reflects on these and many more things besides. I will not go into them, for as I intend to teach you what order is, I may exceed moderation, the source of order. Little by little the soul is led to good habits and a happy life not just by faith, but also by reason. He who has gone into the power and strength of number will find it most unworthy and regrettable on the one hand to apply knowledge to making verse and playing musical instruments, and on the other hand to lead an incongruous lifestyle dominated by lust and by the cacophony of vice.

51. Having recollected and ordered itself, now harmonious and beautiful, the soul will dare to look at God as the source and Father of all Truth. Great God, how will those eyes be! How healthy, beautiful, powerful, intent, serene, happy! And what will they see? What indeed? What can we think, suppose, or say?

est illud quod vident? Quid, quaeso? Quid arbitremur, quid aestimemus, quid loquamur? Quotidiana verba occurrunt, et sordidata sunt omnia vilissimis rebus. Nihil amplius dicam, nisi promitti nobis aspectum pulchritudinis, cuius imitatione pulchra, cuius comparatione foeda sunt caetera. Hanc quisquis viderit (videbit autem qui bene vivit, bene orat, bene studet), quando eum movebit cur alius optans habere filios non habeat, alius abundantes exponat, alius oderit nascituros, diligat alius natos; quomodo non repugnet nihil futurum esse, quod non sit apud Deum, ex quo necesse est ordine omnia fieri et tamen non frustra Deum rogari? Postremo, quando iustum virum movebunt aut ulla onera, aut ulla pericula, aut ulla fastidia, aut ulla blandimenta fortunae?

In hoc enim sensibili mundo vehementer considerandum est quid sit tempus et locus, ut quo delectat in parte, sive loci, sive temporis, intelligatur tamen multo esse melius totum cuius illa pars est; et rursus, quod offendit in parte, perspicuum sit homini docto, non ob aliud offendere, nisi quia non videtur totum, cui pars illa mirabiliter congruit: in illo vero mundo intellegibili, quamlibet partem, tamquam totum, pulchram esse atque perfectam.

Dicentur ista latius, si vestra studia sive memoratum istum a nobis, sive alium fortasse breviorem atque commodiorem, ut hortor ac spero, tenere instituerint, atque omnino naviter constanterque tenuerint.

CAPUT XX
Epilogus hortans ad bonam vitam

52. Quod ut nobis liceat, summa opera danda est optimis moribus; Deus enim noster aliter nos exaudire non poterit, bene autem viventes facillime exaudiet. Oremus ergo, non ut nobis divitiae vel honores vel huiusmodi res fluxae atque nutantes et quovis resistente transeuntes, sed ut ea proveniant, quae nos bonos faciant ac beatos. Quae vota ut devotissime impleantur, tibi maxime hoc negotium, mater, iniungimus, cuius precibus indubitanter credo atque confirmo mihi istam mentem Deum dedisse, ut inveniendae veritati nihil omnino praeponam, nihil aliud velim,

Words that come to mind are those of everyday use, all soiled by giving meaning to the vilest things. I will go no further, except to point out that what has been promised to us is the beauty by which things are beautiful themselves by imitation, and ugly by contrast. On contemplating it (by living, praying, and studying well), why should one be bothered how some people remain childless despite desiring children, some expose those they deem in excess, and some yet hate the unborn, while loving children after being born? It will not appear amiss that nothing happens outside God's order, that things necessarily happen according to that order, and that nevertheless one does not pray to God in vain. Finally, how could the burdens, dangers, dislikes, and allurements of fortune shake a just man?

In the material world one must seriously consider the nature of time and place. The point is that a whole is always far more pleasing to understand than the parts of time or place that make it up. Further, any learned person understands that mistakes are committed in analyzing parts precisely because the whole into which they admirably fit escapes attention. But in the world of the mind any part is as beautiful and perfect as the whole to which it belongs.

These things will be dealt with later. I exhort you and hope you will be eager enough to follow the order exposed above, or perhaps a shorter and easier one, but with unfaltering seriousness and perseverance.

TWENTY
Epilogue. Exhortation to a good life.

52. As far as we are concerned, priority must be given to acquiring good habits. Otherwise God will not heed our requests, while He readily listens to those who live a clean life. Let us not ask, then, for wealth or honors or trifles that change and pass away even from those who hold onto them most tenaciously. Let us ask for those things that make us good and happy. That this may be so, mother, we entrust the task to you. There is no doubt in my mind that it was through your prayers that God gave me the resolve not to prefer anything to the search for truth, nor to desire,

nihil cogitem, nihil amem. Nec desino credere nos hoc tantum bonum, quod te promerente concupivimus, eadem te petente adepturos.

Iam vero te, Alypi, quid horter, quid moneam? Qui propterea nimius non es, quia talia quantumvis amare fortasse semper parum, nimium vero nunquam recte dici potest.

Hic ille:

53. Al.– Vere effecisti, inquit, ut memoriam doctissimorum ac magnorum virorum, quae aliquando pro rerum magnitudine incredibilis videbatur, et quotidiana consideratione et ista praesenti quae in te nobis est admiratione, non solum dubiam non habeamus, verum etiam, si necesse sit, de illa iurare possimus. Quid enim? Nobis nonne illa venerabilis ac prope divina, quae iure et habita est et probata Pythagorae disciplina, abs te hodie, nostris etiam pene oculis reserata est? Cum et vitae regulas, et scientiae non tam itinera quam ipsos campos ac liquida aequora, et quod illi viro magnae venerationi fuit, ipsa etiam sacraria veritatis ubi essent, qualia essent, quales quaererent, et breviter et ita plene significasti, ut quamvis suspicemur et credamus tibi esse adhuc secretiora, tamen non absque impudentiam nos putemus, si amplius quidquam flagitandum arbitremur.

54. A. – Accipio ista, inquam, libenter. Neque enim me tam verba tua, quae vera non sunt, quam verus in verbis animus delectat atque excitat. Et bene quod ei mittere statuimus has litteras, qui de nobis solet libenter multa mentiri. Si qui autem alii fortasse legerint, neque hos metuo ne tibi succenseant. Quis enim amantis errori in iudicando non benevolentissime ignoscat? Quod autem Pythagorae mentionem fecisti, nescio quo illo divino ordine occulto tibi in mentem venisse credo. Res enim multum necessaria mihi prorsus exciderat, quam in illo viro (si quid litteris memoriae mandatis credendum est; quamvis Varroni quis non credat?) mirari et pene quotidianis, ut scis, efferre laudibus soleo, quod regendae reipublicae disciplinam suis auditoribus ultimam tradebat iam doctis, iam perfectis, iam sapientibus, iam beatis. Tantos ibi enim fluctus videbat, ut eis nollet committere nisi virum qui et in regendo pene divine scopulos evitaret et, si omnia defecissent, ipse illis

think about, or love anything else. I also believe that we shall get this great good. We came to desire it mostly through your merits; we shall get it through your prayers.

What advice or exhortation can I give you, Alypius? You are not immoderate in the pursuit of such things. No matter how much you love them, this love will always be little, never excessive.

53. Al. – You have succeeded in imprinting in us the indelible memory of the most learned and great men. Because of its extension, such an achievement seemed incredible, but your teaching us and our admiration for you have attained it beyond doubt. We would be ready to swear by it if necessary. What specifically? Haven't you brought before our eyes that venerable and almost divine science of mathematics rightly attributed to and cultivated by Pythagoras? You have expounded to us both his rule of life and not so much the pathways to science as its very fields and crystal-clear seas. You have opened for us the objects of his veneration, where and what they are, what effort they require. You have done it so concisely and fully, that we suspect you know a great deal more. We would consider ourselves lacking in courtesy were we to insist in asking more than that.

54. A. – I must admit you are right. What delights and excites me are not your words, for they are not true. It is the genuine openness of mind I detect in them. And it is as well that we have decided to write all this to Zenobius, who takes great pleasure in flattering us. So if other people come to read this, I expect they will not take offense at what you say. Who would judge the error of a loved one less than benevolently? Your mentioning Pythagoras, by the way, I believe came to your mind by dint of that same order, obscurely known but powerful nonetheless. One thing in fact escaped me. If memory does not fail me, I remember having read in Varro (and who wouldn't trust him?) something which I have always admired of Pythagoras. He used to teach the science of government last of all. He would reserve this for the learned, mature, wise, and happy disciples of his. He saw politics as a rock-strewn sea. He would not allow anyone to navigate there unless he were

fluctibus quasi scopulus fieret. De solo enim sapiente verissime dici potest,

> *Ille velut pelagi rupes immota, resistit* [Virgil, *Aeneid* 7, 586],

et caetera quae luculentis in hanc sententiam versibus dicta sunt. Hic finis disputationis factus est laetisque omnibus et multum sperantibus consessum dimisimus, cum iam nocturnum lumen fuisset illatum.

able either to avoid them or to stand the buffeting of the waves as steadfast as another rock. It is only of the wise that can be said,

> *He stands like an immovable rock in the sea,*

with what follows in the same poem.

Here the debate ended. Night lights were brought, we closed the session and left, all happy and full of hope.

Index